Cabin Fever

Huntsville History | *No. 13*

A Brief Account of the Life and Times of the Builders and Residents of a Small Log Cabin In Walker County

Cabin Fever

The Roberts-Farris Cabin

A Campus, A Cabin, A Community

Second Edition

Edited by Carolina Castillo Crimm, Ph.D.

TRP: The University Press of SHSU
Huntsville, Texas 77341

Library of Congress Cataloging-in-Publication Data
Names: Crimm, A. Carolina Castillo, 1946- editor.
Title: Cabin fever : the Roberts-Farris Cabin: a campus, a cabin, a community / edited by Carolina Castillo Crimm, Ph.D.
Other titles: Roberts-Farris Cabin: a campus, a cabin, a community
Description: Second edition. | Huntsville, Texas : TRP: The University Press of SHSU, [2025] | Series: Huntsville history | "A Brief Account Of the Life and Times Of the Builders and Residents Of a Small Log Cabin In Walker County." | Includes bibliographical references and index.
Identifiers: LCCN 2024046354 (print) | LCCN 2024046355 (ebook) | ISBN 9781680034202 (paperback) | ISBN 9781680034219 (ebook)
Subjects: LCSH: Roberts-Farris Log Cabin (Tex.) | Historic buildings--Conservation and restoration--Texas--Walker County. | Log cabins--Conservation and restoration--Texas--Walker County. | Farris family--Homes and haunts--Texas--Walker County. | Roberts family--Homes and haunts--Texas--Walker County. | Walker County (Tex.)--Buildings, structures, etc. | Walker County (Tex.)--History. | Frontier and pioneer life--Texas--Walker County. | Huntsville (Tex.)--Buildings, structures, etc. | Huntsville (Tex.)--History.
Classification: LCC F392.W24 C33 2025 (print) | LCC F392.W24 (ebook) | DDC 976.4/169--dc23/eng/20241115
LC record available at https://lccn.loc.gov/2024046354
LC ebook record available at https://lccn.loc.gov/2024046355

SECOND EDITION

Cover art by Carolina Castillo Crimm
Author photo by Denton Florian
Cover design by Cody Gates, Happenstance Type-O-Rama
Interior design by Maureen Forys, Happenstance Type-O-Rama

Printed and bound in the United States of America
First Edition Copyright: 2002

TRP: The University Press of SHSU
Huntsville, Texas 77341
texasreviewpress.org

"Cabin Fever" is an expression generally used to define an individual's psychological feeling of restlessness due to a prolonged confinement in close quarters, such as a small cabin.

Our choice of the term, however, is an attempt to capture the intensely focused drive and determination of a group of people who came together to move a cabin and make it live again.

This book is dedicated to all of those whose lives were touched by the cabin and whose blood, sweat, and tears have preserved the cabin and saved it for posterity.

HUNTSVILLE HISTORY

Series Editor: Carolina Castillo Crimm

TRP's Huntsville History series highlights the history, people, and places around Huntsville, TX, including Walker County and the Piney Woods/ East Texas areas.

BOOKS IN THIS SERIES

No. 001—*A Frontier Texas Mercantile: The History of the Gibbs Brothers and Company, Huntsville*, 1841–1940
by Donald R. Walker

No. 002—*Martha Mitchell of Possum Walk Road: Texas Quiltmaker*
by Melvin R. Mason

No. 003—*Have a Seat, Please*
by Don Reid, with John Gurwell

No. 004—*The Wynne Home: Then and Now*
Edited by Betty Burdett, et al.
Photography by David Carpenter

No. 005—*Deadly Betrayal: The Kidnapping and Murder of McKay Everett*
by Paulette Everett-Norman, James W. Marquart, & Janet Mullings

No. 006—*Seed of Villainy: The Hilton Crawford Story*
by Tannie Shannon

No. 007—*Upon this Chessboard of Nights and Days: Voices from Texas Death Row*
Edited by Dana Allen, et al.

No. 008—*Texas Death Row: Reflections of a Different World*
Edited by Jennifer Gauntt, et al.

No. 009—*Resurrecting Trash: Dan Phillips and the Phoenix Commotion*
Edited by Donald R. Bates, et al.

No. 010—*The Enemy Within Never Did Without: German and Japanese Prisoners of War At Camp Huntsville, Texas, 1942–1945*
Edited by Jeffrey L. Littlejohn & Charles H. Ford

No. 011—*Cooking with the Texas Poets Laureate*
Edited by Elizabeth Ethredge, et al.

No. 012—*Mystic Sails, Texas Trails: Captain Grimes, Shanghai Pierce, Range Wars, and Raising Texas*
by Robert Davant & Mickey Herskowitz

No. 013—*Cabin Fever: The Roberts-Farris Cabin (2nd Edition)*
Edited by Carolina Castillo Crimm

CONTENTS

ACKNOWLEDGMENTS

Preserving the Roberts-Farris Cabin has been a labor of love for many people. Thanks are not sufficient to express my appreciation for the support offered by those who volunteered their time and energy to make this book and the cabin a success.

My first words of appreciation must go to the Farris family. Maggie Farris Parker not only donated the cabin and wrote the Introduction, but she also worked tirelessly with Laura Johnston to complete the history of the family. She pressed many friends and family members into service to help with editing and rewrites. Maxia and Keefer Farris gave of themselves unstintingly, checking on us at the site and supplying the lumber, logs, and materials which we needed to complete the project. Stuart Cox, our project supervisor, and Carroll Tharpe, our advisor, were always available to offer their help and advice.

Shawn Lewis, our Main Street Manager, kept us all going throughout the project. He called, prodded, begged and worked hard to convince us to make sure the cabin became a successful part of his Main Street program. Regretfully, we miss his cheerful presence as he has moved on to other areas. He is no longer available to work on the cabin which is now residing at the Sam Houston Memorial Museum and Presidential Library.

Special thanks go to Linda Pease for bringing everyone together on the project under the auspices of the Main Street Board. Linda supported Maggie Parker in her offer of the cabin and accepted the cabin for the City of Huntsville Arts Commission. In spite of many setbacks and challenges, Linda maintained a steadfast determination to bring the cabin into town. She secured permission from John Smither to locate the cabin on the town square and secured funding for the care and upkeep of the grounds.

The project would never have succeeded without the constant and unswerving support of City Manager Bob Hart. Thanks especially to the City of Huntsville work crews whom Shawn cajoled into hauling wood, moving lumber, bringing logs and clearing the site for us. At the university, my sincere thanks to Dr. Richard Payne, Director of Research and Sponsored Programs, without whom Maggie's cabin would still be rotting in the pasture. His contribution of start-up funds allowed us to begin the project and motivated the City to contribute the money to finish the cabin. Dr. Brian Chapman, Dean of Arts and Sciences, has continued to support the project and came out in the August heat to help dedicate the Cabin. As always, my deepest appreciation and thanks to my beloved Dr. James S. Olson, my History Department Chair, and the best boss a person could ever have. He agreed that this would be an education the students would never forget. He was right.

Dr. Patrick Nolan, Director of the Sam Houston Memorial Museum, although hesitant at first, was willing to loan us the one man without whom the whole project would have failed. My most heartfelt thanks go to Mac Woodward, colleague and friend, who has given more "sweat equity" to the project than anyone. This cabin truly belongs to him. It is also thanks to him, first as Mayor of the City of Huntsville, and later as Director of the Sam Houston Memorial Museum, that the cabin was saved from demolition. After ten years of serving the community as a tourist center and store for the sale of local hand-made goods, we were given six weeks to remove the cabin. Through Mac Woodward's efforts, our cabin was moved onto the museum grounds where it remains today.

At the Texas Department of Criminal Justice, Department head Ed Owens brought our plan together by supplying the labor force we so desperately needed. Our special thanks to Senior Warden David Stacks at the Eastham Unit for loaning us Sergeant Neil Smith and his crew who made it all possible.

Kathy Freydenfeldt, my dear friend and editor, has spent many late nights pouring over this manuscript, even contributing a whole bottle of lamp oil to the project. I take credit for any errors, and she can take credit for the polish.

Finally, my love and appreciation are due to my ever-suffering husband, who knew that I would be spending more time on the cabin than on him, and didn't mind too much. Also, for his many tools which were borrowed, lost, ruined or dirtied beyond repair in the process of building the cabin. He saved our lives with the ammonia-scented ice water that really did bring us back from the dead and kept us going to the end.

INTRODUCTION

By Maggie Farris Parker

If a man's destiny is shaped by the company he keeps, then surely a home's history is shaped by the families it has sheltered. Six generations of families have lived in this 160-year-old notched-log cabin. It began back in 1840 with its first owners, Allen and Henrietta Roberts and their nine children. It continued up through World War II when the last inhabitants were the Ernest Brown family.

Throughout all these generations, living standards were primitive. There was no running water, gas, telephone, or electricity. The entire family slept, cooked, ate and lived in this one 324- square foot room for many years. Eventually, at some undetermined date, a kitchen shed was added on the back. Later still, shed rooms for sleeping were added to each side, and later the family added a front porch. These additions, then, more than doubled the living space.

Allen Roberts was one of the early settlers in the new Republic of Texas. He had joined his stepfather and mother, Hezekiah and Matilda Faris, in their journey down from Tennessee. These two families, as well as several other families in the group, resolved to stake a claim in this new territory. They did so at a site along the headwaters of the east fork of the San Jacinto River, in what is now Walker County. They named their new community "Goshen" in memory of the area they had left in Tennessee. Their focus was very much like that of most of the early pioneers moving westward: to tame and domesticate the wilderness.

For most of their lives, these early pioneers were engaged in the back-breaking work of clearing virgin forests, draining bogs, and planting and harvesting crops. Fatal accidents were not uncommon among the men. Infant mortality was high, and wives and mothers not infrequently died by their early forties, their deaths attributed to too many children too close together. In addition, there were other physically demanding chores for a typical pioneer's wife—cooking, washing, the care and milking of the cows, and the responsibility of the garden. From it they canned or dried fruits and vegetables to last the family through the winter months. Pantries were filled with whatever was produced or grown on that farm. Settlers traveled by horseback or in a wagon pulled by mules. Medical help was from home remedies. In special instances, they might have the help of a midwife, or rarely, from a medical doctor.

Although each particular family who lived in this cabin had its own unique characteristics, there is no doubt that tragedy, suffering and sacrifice, heroism and difficulties beset each and every one of them. The stories which are told in this book, some factual, others by conjecture, will help us all to visualize the hardships and danger from a difficult time, an inhospitable environment, and occasional raids.

The cabin itself has been changed over the years. At some point in the cabin's history, newspapers were pasted to the interior of the logs to help stop the cold north wind from whistling through the cracks. The evidence of such a practice was the ragged snippets of newspaper found wrapped around some of the nail heads at the time of the cabin's removal into the town square of Huntsville. Other evidence of a long-ago tenant family with very little income was the fifteen-inch-high chicken-wire Christmas tree whose spaces were stuffed with small pinecones and brightened by three or four tiny balls, no longer colored, no longer shiny. This treasure was pulled from beneath the cabin at the time of its move.

Tradition has it that Roberts granted, or sold, the cabin to his stepbrother, James Morgan Faris. It has been passed down through the next four generations of Faris progeny, during which time the name was changed to Farris. On several occasions, the cabin was moved from one location to another on Faris (Farris) land holdings in order to better accommodate sharecroppers and later tenant farmers.

In the early 1930s, James H. Farris gave the cabin to his son, Alton. They disassembled the cabin and moved it by mule power, one more time, to a hillside overlooking Sandy Creek on the Alton Farris farm. A new tenant and his family were ready to move in and begin their farming duties as sharecroppers.

With the beginning of World War II and the return of prosperity, the small cabin in the pasture was converted into a hay barn. Over the years, cows wandered through it, finding shelter within it walls from cold winter winds. The termites and dry rot began taking their toll. In time, the cabin would have slowly disintegrated as so many cabins have done throughout Texas. The Farris family, however, was determined that the cabin should continue as a reminder to future generations of the efforts of their ancestors.

The original structure was moved to a site on the Huntsville main square. This effort was undertaken so that future generations may have the opportunity to relive some of the history of a people who lived so long ago. The intent is that they will gain, thereby, a better appreciation for the tragedy, suffering and sacrifice, the heroism and difficulty with which our commonwealth was carved out of the wilderness.

The time finally came in August 2001. Maggie, Truett, Keefer, and Maxia, descendants of Hezekiah Farris, and the children of Alton and Erma Farris, presented to the City of Huntsville and the citizens of Walker County, this relic of our collective past. It was, and is, our hope that this Roberts-Farris cabin, another link in the chain of authentic buildings from the days of the Republic of Texas, will help draw ever new groups of children, youth, and adults to the historic city of Huntsville.

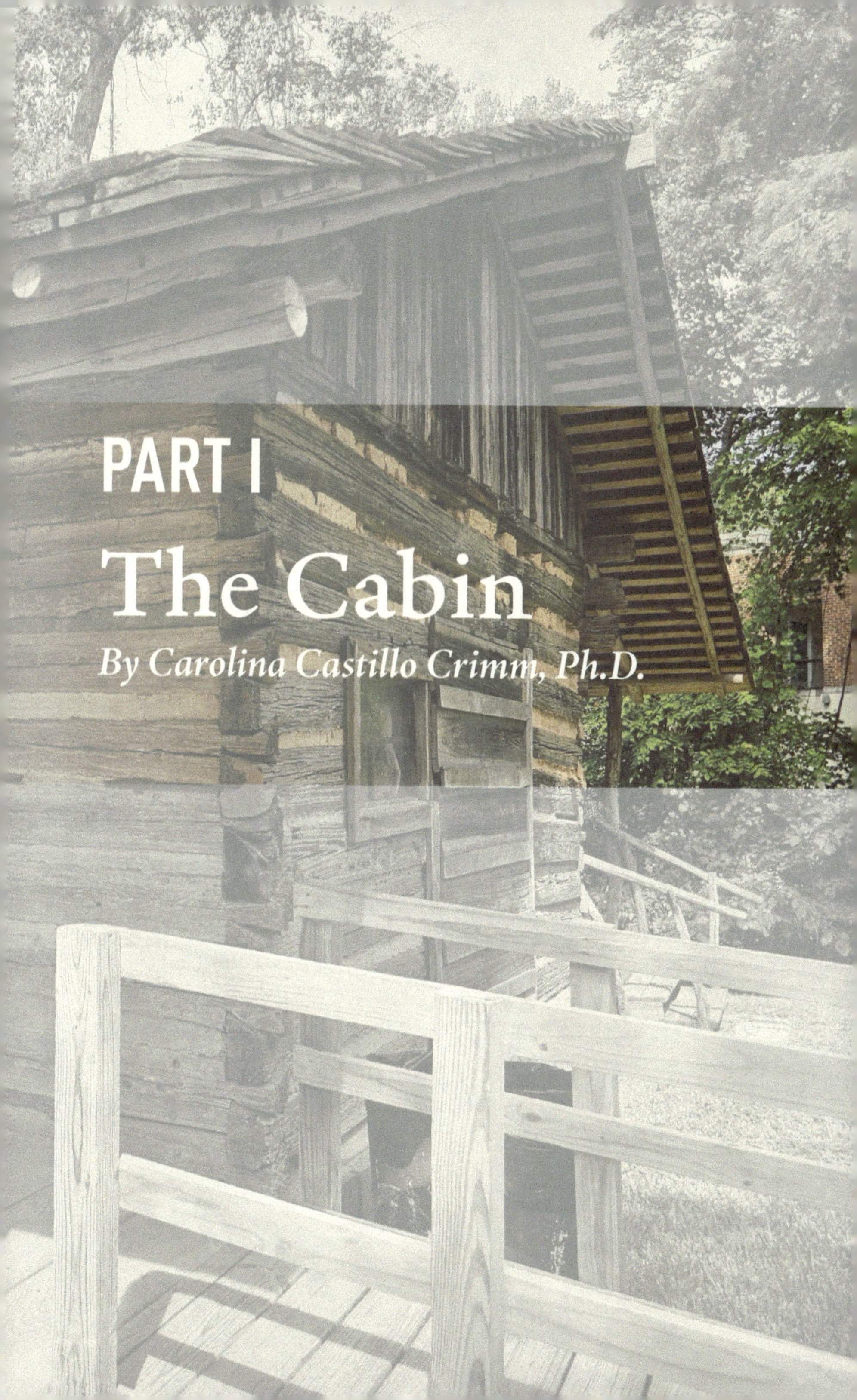

PART I

The Cabin

By Carolina Castillo Crimm, Ph.D.

CHAPTER 1

The Characters

"Of course the two Texas History classes can move a log cabin! We'll have an undergraduate and graduate class and a couple of weeks during a summer course. That should be plenty of time to dismantle the cabin, move it into town, restore the logs, reassemble the building, and rebuild the roof. How hard can it be? Sort of like Lincoln Logs, don't you think? We'll have about thirty students, most of them future teachers, many of them big, brawny wannabe-coaches. The graduate class can do the research and write reports on the history of the cabin. Then we'll publish a little book about the whole project. I'm sure the students will be excited to have the chance to do something so historic!"

Comments by Dr. Carolina Crimm to Commissioner Linda Pease, Spring, 2001.

It sounded like such a plausible little project. A simple cabin, a few logs to stack up, then just move that cute little cabin to the town square. Isn't naivete a wonderful thing? Linda Pease, director of the Huntsville Arts Commission, was to blame from the beginning. Linda, a lovely, slender woman of medium height with sparkly green eyes and beautiful white hair cut in an elegant pageboy. Little did I know she was also a quietly determined advocate of difficult causes, a long-time resident and Cultural Services Coordinator for Huntsville. For more than twenty years, Linda was dedicated to improving Huntsville's downtown.

A cabin has been a part of the Master Plan for Huntsville's downtown since at least 1990. At that time, Linda combined the efforts of artist Richard Haas and Kim A. Williams, AIA, to produce a master plan for Huntsville, based on historic preservation and architectural illusion paintings. The cabin under consideration was the Roberts-Farris cabin, thought to be the oldest log cabin in Walker County. The plan was to place it on the historic site of Pleasant Gray's Trading Post, at that time an empty lot on the downtown square belonging to sixth-generation resident John Smither. Maggie Farris Parker, the owner of the cabin, had hoped for many years that the cabin could be saved. In 1990, she offered to donate the cabin to the city. By 2001, when nothing had been done, she added an incentive of $1,000 to complete the project.

Ever the energetic optimist, Linda Pease spent years working on saving the cabin. She visited, evaluated and photographed it. She wrote up a decision package to send to the City Council, requesting approval and funds. At the time, Huntsville's leadership maintained an austere point of view that the role of government was to protect the citizenry, supply water, collect garbage, and stay out of everything else. The Council turned her requests down, but Linda continued to submit the proposal year after year.

In February 2000, Huntsville hired Bob Hart as the new City Manager. He had just left Georgetown, Texas, one of the best examples of what a Main Street Program can do. When Hart arrived in Huntsville, among the first words out of his mouth were, "You all need to be a Main Street town."

The Texas Main Street Program, supported by the Texas Historical Commission (THC), is based on the National Main Street Center Program of the National Trust for Historic Preservation. The National Trust is "a leading advocate of preservation in the United States." It is dedicated to "economic growth, urban revitalization, and the creation of new jobs . . . through the rehabilitation of historic structures." (THC, Main Street Board Training brochure, Austin, p. 1)

Cities in Texas apply for participation in the Main Street program through the Texas Historical Commission. Three to six applicants are selected each year. Linda Pease, by now an accomplished grant writer, applied, and Huntsville was accepted.

The THC offers three years' assistance in the restoration and preservation of the downtown area to cities which receive the Main Street designation. Those cities can continue to receive help from the state of Texas for an additional three years. It was up to Bob Hart and Mayor Bill Green to hire a Main Street Manager.

The new hire would establish a Program Advisory Committee and appoint local citizens to committees in the areas of design, promotion, economic restructuring and organization. The success of the Main Stret Program depended almost entirely on the success of the new manager. Dozens of people applied. The interview committee narrowed down more than thirty applicants to nine interviewees. Of those, one young man stood out above all the rest. His name was Shawn Lewis.

The tall, lanky, good-looking, sandy haired young West Texan drove into town from Abilene in January of 2001. Shawn was born and raised on a ranch in Gail, Texas, where his father, appropriately enough, was Sheriff of Borden County. Two years at Pepperdine University in California working on a master's degree in public policy had mellowed his West Texas drawl. A stint of work in Abilene as management assistant to the City Manager, however, had not affected his cheerful exuberance. He came into Huntsville ready to make miracles happen.

Shawn Lewis and Linda Pease became a dynamic, practically steamroller, combination. I was a history professor at Sam Houston State University at the time, with a Master's in Architectural Preservation. Impressed with the ideas of the Main Street program, I volunteered to join the board and met Shawn and Linda in the early Spring of 2001.

Dedicated as always, Linda brought up the subject of Maggie's historic cabin and the possibility of moving it downtown. Shawn thought it was a wonderful idea and the two community leaders began discussing methods of carrying out their ideas. Infected by their enthusiasm and caught up in the excitement of the moment, I mentioned that I would be teaching two Texas History courses during the summer. One would be an undergraduate class with many future history teachers. The second class was a graduate class with older students who would, without doubt, love the historical aspects of such a class. Without meaning any harm to myself or others, I said, "Why, sure we can move the cabin!"

No one knew, for sure, if the cabin could be moved, much less if it could be done in the constricted time frame that a five-week summer course gave us. Before we even considered actually moving it, we needed to carry out a survey of the cabin, inspect it for damage and determine whether, how, or even *if* we might accomplish this feat in the allotted time.

In March, several of us gathered to drive out to the pasture to inspect the cabin. We also realized that in order to pull off this miracle, we were going to need a lot of help. By this time, our team had come to include far more than Linda, Shawn, and I.

The first additions to the team were our leaders, two of the Farris brothers—Keefer, the eldest, and Maxia, the youngest. Maggie Farris Parker, their elder sister and donor of the cabin, lived in distant Houston and did not attend our inspection, although she was keenly interested.

Keefer, at seventy-some, was graying, wiry, wrinkled, and constantly on the go in his blue coveralls. He was always up at three in the morning, mowing lawns, planting trees, fixing equipment and running errands for his long-time employers, the Gibbs Brothers Lumber Company. He was familiar with the hundreds of acres of forests on the Gibbs properties. With the support of the sixth-generation Gibbs heirs, he offered to help us replace any logs that might be rotted or broken.

Keefer's brother, Maxia, equally sinewy and spare, with a dry, feisty sense of humor, had experience in construction and restoring old buildings. He became our supervisor, and if we needed help of any kind, he was always on hand to offer solutions. More than that, he actually became involved in the day-to-day work on the cabin.

James Patton, Walker County Clerk for more than twenty years, served as the Chair of the Walker County Historical Commission. He supported us from a distance, not certain of the success of our project but willing to help if he could. He provided Linda with the early photographs of the Roberts-Farris cabin. He agreed that it was very probably the oldest remaining cabin in the county. His own extended family had resided in Walker County for at least five generations. Because of his encyclopedic knowledge of the many ramifications of his own family, and every other family in the county, James Patton could almost always find some degree of kinship with everyone he met.

We were also blessed with two local preservation experts: Carroll Tharpe and Stuart Cox. Carroll, a retired Registered Architect and Fellow in Historic Preservation, was a slight, gray- haired gentleman, crippled by youthful polio but completely unhindered by his disability. His passion for the past thirty years had been the restoration of historic buildings.

While serving on the Committee on Historic Resources for the American Institute of Architects, he and his lovely, petite wife, Mae, began collecting log cabins and nineteenth- century buildings. Frequently working without help, the two of them documented, marked, dismantled, and moved almost a dozen buildings to their fifty-acre property in Montgomery County. Over the years they learned as they built and willingly shared their knowledge with us.

Our other preservationist was Stuart Cox, a stocky, bluff, good-hearted German American with a deep and boisterous laugh. He admitted that he was the bane of his wife's existence, frequently getting caught up in projects and forgetting to go home for meals. Although completely self-taught, Stuart has long been known in Huntsville as an accomplished carpenter and furniture restoration expert. Over the years, he has become an authority on early Texas furniture and pottery, ceramic jugs in particular. His interest in antique furniture expanded to include nineteenth century hand tools. He believed in repairing old furniture with tools from the same period. His interest in furniture also led to rebuilding and repairing several nineteenth century log cabins. Like the Tharpes, he learned by doing, and like them, he became our mentor and guide.

From the Sam Houston Memorial Museum, we acquired Dr. Patrick Nolan, Museum Director, and Mac Woodward, the Museum Curator. Pat was a bearded, bespectacled, jolly, Yankee transplant. He began his career as a history professor at Wisconsin, River Falls, then turned to museum work. He served as Director at the Wright State Museum in Dayton, Ohio, then at the Hagley Museum and Library in Delaware before coming to Sam Houston Memorial Museum in 1992.

Mac Woodward stood well over six feet, a typical, quiet, soft-spoken Texan. His pedigree goes back to 1841 when the Gibbs family helped found Huntsville. Much of his interest in the history of the cabin stemmed from the Gibbs Mercantile archives which includes letters from Sam Houston and bills of sale to the original families.

Mac had the strength and determination to inspire us all and made him the linchpin for the whole project. Like Pat, he did not begin in museum work but in history. He received his B.A. in History at Sam Houston State University and his M.A. at the University of Houston. When a job opened in the Education Division at the museum, Mac stepped in. He grew with the job, rising to Curator of Collections where he was part of the museum's effort to upgrade and become accredited. He attended numerous seminars in preservation, as well as graduating from the Modern Archives Institute in Washington, D. C. Of us all, he was the best trained and best prepared to take on the cabin project.

The most decisive member of the inspection team was Howard Long, the building mover. Howard, dour, silent and solid, his crumpled whitish-gray cowboy hat always firmly attached to his head, had spent his life moving buildings. He had cut buildings in half, in thirds, even in quarters, and hauled them halfway across Texas. If he said we could move the cabin, then we could move the cabin.

March in Texas is invariably wet and pastures are notoriously boggy. The little cabin sat high on a slope overlooking a low-lying pasture. The pasture, once a swamp, was drained by a small creek known as the West Sandy. To get to the cabin, we had to negotiate our way across the rutted, mucky road and up the long hill. On that early Saturday morning, Linda and Shawn invited those interested in the cabin to meet at the site to consider our options.

People in Texas who drive pickup trucks do so for a very good reason—muddy pastures being one of those reasons. Without access to our own truck, Linda and I, in her four-door Volvo sedan, with Carroll and Mae Tharpe in the back seat, set off to find the cabin. We finally located the gate to the Farris property, after back-tracking only once.

As Linda and I drove in, we could see half a dozen pickups parked next to the cabin high on the hill in the distance. The road, churned up by the passage of the many trucks into a quagmire, was clearly impassable for our little sedan. We considered walking but Linda, ever game, was certain she could make it. Hands gripping the wheel, she headed into the mud. She never let her foot off the accelerator. With the wheels spinning, mud flying in rooster tails behind us, we skidded across the pasture, bounced over the ruts, slithered our way up the hill, and finally slid to a stop beside the pickups. Carroll, Mae and I let out our collective breaths and gratefully crawled out of her Volvo. All of us, in particular the men, joined in giving Linda a laughing, standing ovation.

The men, including Shawn, Pat Nolan, Mac Woodward, Stuart Cox, and James Patton were already clambering around the cabin. Carroll and I joined then, stepping hesitantly through the smelly muck, a mixture of manure and acrid cow urine, into the dusky interior. Inside, a high, almost cathedral-like ceiling stretched thirty feet or more into the darkness above us. The interior was surprisingly large. It appeared to be almost twenty feet on a side. I stumbled over deep piles of what looked like dusty, moldy hay. Thin strips of lath had been nailed over the chinks between the logs, so that little light or air entered the room except through the three small doors and the opening from a burned-out fireplace.

Most cabins of this period are built of rounded logs. Early pioneers often did not have the time or the skill to hand-hew each log. In addition, rounded logs shed water better when there was no overhang. As I laid my hand on the rough surface of the logs, I could feel the regular adze marks on the wood. It was obvious that this cabin was different. The early builder's skill was evident in the smooth, squared off sides of the logs. Whoever he was, he had scored each of the massive twenty-foot logs with an axe, then used the adze, a tool like an axe but with an offset head which allowed the builder to chisel away the rounded edges. Each log was perfectly flat on all four sides. In each corner, half-dovetail notches were carefully and precisely cut, locking each log securely into its neighbor. I pushed against the logs. The little cabin felt rock-solid.

Embedded in the logs were nails with bits of paper still clinging to them. The last inhabitant, according to Keefer, had been an African American tenant family during the 1940s. They had tacked thick layers of newspapers to the walls to provide insulation for the cabin's residents.

Over the years, whoever the tenants were who had lived there and farmed the land, had added rooms and porches to all four sides and built a corrugated metal roof over the cabin. That protection had saved the cabin logs. During the depths of the Great Depression, Keefer's father had roofed one of the porches with 1933 license plates, available from the Huntsville prison where they had been manufactured. The license plates, although rusted, were still clearly legible. A stray trumpet vine, thick with age, had grown up along one porch and draped bright orange blossoms across the rusty roof. Sturdy bois d'arc trees (that's "bow-dark" for the French term for the sturdy trees that the early natives used for bows), had intertwined their roots and branches with the porches.

Cows had occupied the pasture, and the cabin too, it appeared. The last human tenant had left close to sixty years earlier. What I had stumbled over inside was the hay that had been kept in the cabin. The cows, without doors to bar their path, had entered and helped themselves, leaving evidence of their stay. Cow patties (a Southern euphemism for cow manure) had mixed with the hay, turning gradually to dusty heaps, as much as twelve to fifteen inches deep across the entire inside of the cabin. Removing the smelly piles would be no easy task.

As we gathered outside the cabin, everyone had questions and opinions. Could we move it? Should we move it intact or disassemble it? Was it worth saving? It was hard to tell the condition of the lower logs of the cabin, since the porch floors hid much of the base. We could see that termites and wood rot had crumbled at least parts of the base logs.

A fire had damaged one opening, evidently where a fireplace had once stood. The blackened logs, still secured to the side walls by their half dovetail notches, had sagged downward at the center, no longer supported by the beams of the fireplace. If the cabin were moved, the logs would have to be secured somehow. The remaining three doorjambs were still intact, and they would serve to hold the walls.

What were the options? Carroll Tharpe, hobbling around the cabin, opted for dismantling and reassembling the logs after they had been treated with preservatives and fillers. It was the sensible thing to do. If the logs remained locked together, and the cabin were moved as a unit, he said, replacing the rotten lower logs would be almost impossible.

Stuart Cox, with his German problem-solving persistence, suggested that if the cabin were moved as a whole, once in town, we could slide heavy sheets of steel between the logs; place jacks under each side and lift the upper logs so that the lower ones could be replaced.

Howard Long silently circled the cabin and stood back, eyeing his adversary. With enough I-beams, enough braces, enough plywood nailed to hold the logs in place. He nodded silently—if we wanted it moved, he could move it. Only 2,500 bucks. A thousand from Maggie, but where would the other $1,500 come from? Naively confident, I believed the money would appear from somewhere.

James Patton, Mac Woodward, and Pat Nolan stood back and just shook their heads. Pat and Mac looked at each other. They were thankful the little cabin was not going to end up as a pile of trash on the museum grounds.

The problem was time. A summer school course only lasts five weeks, each class an hour and a half long. We needed some lectures to tie the history of the cabin into our textbook, a few readings and discussions to provide a basis for understanding the lives of the people who had occupied the cabin. And, of course, the requisite two tests, a midterm and final although the students would have been happy to do without those.

Working on the cabin would be counted for credit, and the students would work on it whenever they could fit it into their schedules. We could squeeze in only a day or two for dismantling the porches and removing the roof. If Howard Long could move the cabin to the town square on Saturday, we could spend the following week, during our class time, reroofing the cabin and at least getting it dried in. There was no time for preservation. The cabin would be rough, but it would be usable, or so I believed. Again, James, Mac, and Pat just shook their heads. Linda never admitted it, but chances are she was losing confidence.

Now the problem was money. University administrators are usually sensible, level-headed, conservative businessmen. The university is, after all, a very large business. Who would be crazy enough to fund a harebrained scheme such as moving a historic cabin? And what on earth for? Where was the economic benefit to the university?

I typed up a proposal. I knew we needed Howard's $1,500 and probably another thousand or two to publish the book. Then the cost of stabilizers for the cabin, preservatives for the logs, transportation, food, and drink for the students out at the site. And, of course, the requisite T-shirts. Truthfully, I had no idea what all the money would be needed for. I had never moved a cabin before. I asked for $5,000 and sent the request up the chain of command.

My immediate boss, History Department Chair, Dr. James Olson is always supportive of his professors, no matter how crazy our ideas. If the students will benefit, he is for it. He never doubted us or our project. He signed the proposal and sent it along.

Dr. Brian Chapman, the Dean of Arts and Sciences, is a quiet sensible man, frugal and careful of the university's money. To my surprise, he caught the vision. He realized, far more than I, what the cabin might mean to both the university and the community. He agreed to my proposition but shook his head regretfully. He did not have the money to give me.

With his approval, the memo went up the chain to the Vice President for Academic Affairs. Dr. David Payne also approved, but he too did not have extra funds to support the project. He signed it and sent the proposal on.

The request finally landed on the desk of the Associate Vice President for Research and Sponsored Programs at SHSU, Dr. Richard Payne (no relation to the vice president). Dr. Payne was a big man, towering six foot six, with a gruff, deep voice, a close-cropped white beard and a frightening presence. He had served as Department Chair for Political Science for many years. When students first met him, they trembled in terror. I, too, hesitated before his scrutiny. For those who got to know him, however, Dick Payne's tough exterior hid a kindly, caring interior.

Dick Payne believed very strongly in supporting the efforts of deserving faculty. The hard sciences, known for their glamorous, splashy projects, often received hundreds of thousands of dollars of start-up money. People in the humanities and social sciences, on the other hand, rarely get funded at all.

He felt it was very important for the Research Office to finance those who did not have a natural, science-backed, support network. He agreed that my project had merit, not realizing that he would receive commendations from colleges across the country for his efforts on my behalf. The money to move the cabin came from his coffers, all $5,000 of it. It looked like the cabin could become a reality.

Now Shawn and Linda had to find a place to put the cabin. We considered using the small Founder's Park, a block off the town square. The property belonged to the city, but then we would be bound by city codes and regulations. By June, Shawn began negotiations with John Smither, of the Robert Smither Estate, to use the vacant lot between two of the Smither buildings on University Avenue, facing the Courthouse.

After a month of negotiating, Shawn had secured a verbal agreement from the Smither heirs to allow the city to lease the premises for ten years, beginning on August 1, 2001. In exchange, Shawn and Linda had gotten the city to pay the taxes on the property, and to provide liability insurance.

Seven of the parking spots behind the lot had been leased to the tenants of the two adjoining buildings. They would continue to have free use of their parking facilities. The only other requirement was the inclusion of the name Smither on whatever signage was used. Shawn had succeeded where no one had thought he would. Although the document would still have to go through another month of wrangling, the cabin had a place to live.

Workers were the next hurdle. I've always believed in the ant theory. Following the song about the ants and rubber tree plants, I knew that with enough ants—or students—we could move anything.

Students, bless their little souls, are at the mercy of whatever administrative whim places a professor at the head of their classrooms. Rumors abound about which teachers to take and which to avoid. The internet even provides a "pick-a-prof" site with comments from students about their likes and dislikes about professors. Choosing classes is often about the professors, but sometimes a scheduling conflict means that students have no choice. They are stuck with taking classes with "Terrible" Turlington or "Flunk'em" Flannigan. I was rather proud of the nickname which I learned that my student had blessed me with. I was the "Crimm Reaper."

Texas History is required of all students planning to be history teachers. Since I was the only professor teaching Texas History that summer, the students had no choice. Those who signed up for History 439 that summer of 2001 were stuck with the "Crimm Reaper." Little did they, or I, know that I just might earn that name in more ways than just grades. That summer class was made up of thirty-two students, about evenly split between male and female. Most were seniors and mostly history majors or minors. Several of the young men, as was usually the case with this class, were planning to go into coaching with history as a teaching field. That meant that they were large, brawny young men.

I dropped the bomb the first day. I handed out the syllabus in which I had included what I called "an Opportunity."

> *"This summer as part of our Texas History class, you will have an opportunity to be part of a historic Huntsville event. The Farris Cabin, the oldest cabin in Walker County, has been donated by the family to the city. It will be moved to a site on the downtown square. The Walker County Historical Commission and the city Administration have invited us to be involved in moving and restoring this small cabin"*

I went on to describe the cabin. I explained what the students would learn from the project and what would be involved. The plan sounded simple enough. "Students will spend a week in the field dismantling the side sheds and roof under the supervision of two preservation architects."

At least I hoped Carroll Tharpe and Stuart Cox might stop by to check on our progress. I went on: "Members of the undergraduate Texas History class during the second summer session will rebuild the roof and dry-in the cabin."

That is the nice thing about being a teacher. Years of indoctrination have conditioned students to believe that teachers know what they are doing. When you assure students, with utter self-confidence, that something can be done, the students believe it. And when a teacher tells them to sign up, they obey. It really is an amazing social phenomenon. I concluded with:

> *"This is an exciting and tremendously worthwhile project that will benefit the community and the university while preserving the history of our county. It is, without doubt, a history course you will never forget. I look forward to your participation in this rewarding adventure."*

The only thing I was truly sure of was that it would indeed be unforgettable.

The students looked at each other, a few with raised eyebrows, rolled eyes and knowing looks. "We've got another nut case for a teacher!" Some of the students did not show up the following day and I did get four drop slips. But the majority decided to stick it out, whether out of a need for the course, or raw courage, or maybe mere curiosity.

The second Texas History class was a graduate class: History 589. Most of the students were working on Master's degrees. In the syllabus, graduate students were expected to choose a topic and prepare a ten-to-fifteen-page paper from primary research. It should deal with the cabin, the family, the land, or the society of the period.

Graduate classes are always a mixed bag, and this class was no exception. First was Laura Johnson, a pert, cheerful petite white-haired lady in glasses. I realized with a sinking sensation why she seemed so familiar. I had seen her at the undergraduate graduation the year before. At eighty-four, she was the oldest graduate from Sam

Houston State University. Here she was in my class, and I was expecting her to go out in hundred-degree heat and help dismantle a cabin! As the "Crimm Reaper" I might well earn my nickname. She was game, however, and seemed excited about the prospect. She chose the Farris family as her report topic.

The second shock was Dr. Ross Lovell. An elegant, trim gentleman in his sixties with white hair and a neatly clipped moustache. Dr. Lovell had just retired from the University's School of Business with the prestige of a Full Professor. He had signed up for the Texas History class just to learn a little more about Texas. He wanted to have something to do with his spare time during retirement. I never imagined that a man of his stature would stoop to anything so menial as getting his hands dirty helping with the manure in the cabin. Like Laura, however, Ross was delighted to be included.

David Parnell, a middle School Social studies teacher from Centerville, was in his fifties. Tall and taciturn, he had a graying beard and grizzled hair. His looks were deceiving. We learned he was a dynamic teacher. Although quiet, he was willing to try anything. David was looking forward to finishing his master's degree and teaching at a junior college to complete his career. I was relieved to find that he was as dedicated to the cabin as the others.

In the graduate class, I found my right-hand woman. Susan Locklear rounded out the elders in the class. She had always wanted to be a teacher. As a single mom, however, she had to work to put her two boys through college, before taking time out for her own education. She was already going gray, although she was relatively young. She proved to be effervescent, always upbeat, an overachiever and willing to do anything that needed doing. More than that, she was bright, always thinking one step ahead, resolving problems before they arose. There was no doubt that she would make a great teacher, but for me, she became my support and confidante, always there to help when I needed her. I was very pleased to learn that she did go on to receive numerous awards for her teaching.

The remainder of the graduate class were students in their twenties. They were the typical, dedicated, driven grad students and future historians. Thomas Vanderberg, Randy White, and Kristina McCoy had only one semester left to complete their master's degree. They were more interested in getting their papers done and moving on than worrying about a silly cabin. Like all of us, however, they came to take pride in the little cabin.

We spent the first two weeks in the undergraduate class reading the textbook, covering Texas history, and laying the background for our foray into the wilds. The students read Terry Jordan's book on log cabins, and Jo Ella Exley Powell's *Texas Tears and Texas Sunshine.* The first autobiography in Powell's book, the story of Mary Blankenship, carried the students right into the heart of the 1840s.

Mary and her husband had come from Tennessee to Texas, and here he had built a small log cabin for Mary and her two children. When her husband went off to search for another homesite, Mary was left in the cabin to feed and care for the children. Alone, she chopped wood for the cooking fire, dragged buckets of water up the hill from the creek for the laundry, tended to the small garden, and provided for the pigs that grunted and rooted in the cool earth under the cabin.

At night, her greatest fear were the natives she heard prowling around the cabin in the dark. To still her own terror, she spent sleepless nights spinning thread by the noisy whir of her wheel. That story of the lonely woman in the cabin deeply affected the students, especially when they saw our cabin on the hill the following week.

CHAPTER 2

Moving the Cabin

I had begun to plan the move with a touch of trepidation. I was facing thirty-some wary undergraduate students, seven cynical graduate students, the Mayor, the City Manager, the entire city staff, and the university administration, to say nothing of the Museum staff. I had to pretend I knew what I was doing. I didn't, but I did have Linda Pease for moral support and Shawn to prod me along and to supervise.

My initial plans were to take the students out to the site on Friday, July 20th. Shawn and I had been back out to the cabin. We realized that we could not possibly remove all the sheds and the roof in one day. That was not a problem—I extended the workdays. I told the students we would be going out on Thursday as well. Since many of the students had jobs, or were taking other classes, I passed around a sign-up sheet broken down by jobs and times.

The three teams were Roof Removal, Removal of Sheds, and Food and Water. The shifts were every two hours from eight in the morning to four in the afternoon. I told them to bring hats, work gloves, comfortable clothes, sturdy shoes, sunscreen lotion, hammers, hand tools, and friends to help.

There was no question of "if." It was a class assignment and worth 600 points, the same as the two tests. Those who were "physically challenged" were assigned to the food committee. The rest became the worker ants. The excitement was rising. They didn't even complain. What other history class had such an unusual field trip? They signed up.

July in Texas is hot. There is no way around it. There was one advantage, however, the mud of our March visit was gone. The road across the pasture was rutted, rough and dry as a bone. Another problem was the absence of shade around the cabin. Shawn, bless him, found two canopies and brought them to the site on Thursday morning.

I borrowed my husband's pickup truck and loaded it with everything I could think of from my husband's horde of tools. I loaded the truck with ice chests, coolers, tables, ground tarpaulins, ladders, claw hammers, sledgehammers, both chain and hand saws, crowbars, pry bars, and anything else I could find in our garage. I admit that not all of his tools came back!

My husband had told me about a trick he learned while playing ball in the Texas summer heat. Their team had added a small bottle of spirits of ammonia to a bucket of ice water. The ammonia is still available in some drug stores. He and his teammates wiped their faces with the cloths dipped in the icy liquid. More effective than any aroma therapy, the ammonia water could very nearly revive the dead. He was right. It did.

The Food and Water teams, Rick Erck and Sarah Hall were given assignments. Food for the crew consisted of 150 kolaches, five dozen doughnuts, one hundred bottles of water, one hundred bottles of Gatorade, ten bags of ice, one large fruit tray, and twenty orange juice bottles. Lunch consisted of an order of thirty Subway sandwiches, chips and cookies to be picked up at noon.

The team felt particularly appreciated when they arrived with the food and were cheered by the teams. They stocked the ice chests, kept the coolers replenished, brought lunch, and cleaned up the trash afterward. In the ferocious heat we drank every drop of liquid and had to send for more.

Lynette Nadeau also showed up early. One of the nontraditional students, she was a single mother with two teenagers. Lynette was a cheerful, bustling, chipper, officious, can-do kind of mother. She is of medium height, with dark, curly hair and a happy smile. She is also a registered Emergency Medical Technician. She adopted all of us as hers. For the full course of the project, she checked to make sure we had enough water. We heard "Have you had enough water?" "Drink more water." "Come down off that roof and have some water." "Time for a water break." "Here, come have some Gatorade." "Remember to rehydrate." Followed by stories of people who had fainted or gone into comas from not having enough water. We did as "mother" ordered, and no one fainted from dehydration.

Students are not noted for being early risers. It wasn't until ten a.m. that we had a contingent of about fifteen or twenty students at the site. They were making huge inroads into the doughnuts and kolaches. I called them together and showed them the four porches which had to be removed. Siding, flooring, posts, and roofs—all of it had to come off. We parceled out the sledgehammers, axes and prybars. My neatly planned schedule and sign-up sheet went out the window.

Young people—male or female, it seems to make no difference—love to rip and tear and pull things apart. It may be the feeling of power in destroying something. They launched into that building like an end-of-semester party. Nails screeched as the students applied the prybars. They swung hammers against the ancient siding, ripped up the flooring and tore off walls. As the sun rose in the clear blue sky, the once-quiet pasture echoed with their shouts of laughter.

Outside the cabin, the *bois d'arc* trees had to be removed. David Parnell, the grad student, had brought his chain saw. He paired off with one of the future coaches, Darren Jones, who had never used a chain saw but was willing to learn. The two of them attacked the thick trees that held up the porches. They soon learned why the natives had used the wood for their tough hunting bows.

David's chain saw bogged down almost immediately. The wood resisted as if it were made of some strange impenetrable rubber. As David pressed harder, the spinning saw teeth bit deeper into the wood. Suddenly, the blade hit a knot and the chainsaw twisted out of his hand. Without pressure on the trigger, the chain stopped but the heavy handle dropped with a crunching thud right on top of David's foot. Score one for the *bois d'arc*, and a wounded warrior for us. With Darren's help, David retreated to Lynette's van. There she propped his foot up, checked to make sure it was not broken and covered it with ice and provided David with aspirin.

Without the chain saw, we would have to use axes. Several of the "macho" young men volunteered immediately. One of the volunteers, who shall remain nameless, was the kicker for our Sam Houston Bearkats. Only later did a friend remind me that our university football coach would have found out his prize kicker had been using an axe to attack the rubbery wood, thus threatening his own existence and the fate of the football season. It was not the kicker who nearly bought the ranch.

The axes had not made a dent, bouncing off the wood with each attempted cut. A very large, muscular young man, without a doubt a future football coach, swung the axe at the tree with all the force he could muster. Being new to the axe-wielding game, he misjudged the distance to the tree. The head of the axe missed but the handle hit with deadly force. The blow splintered the handle, and the steel head of the axe came spinning off around the tree. The flying missile just missed his arm leaving him shaking with the close call. Score two for the *bois d'arc* and another wounded warrior for mother to care for.

We did eventually defeat the *bois d'arc* but it took us the rest of the day. Darren Jones was the only one left to run the chain saw. With uncommon courage after David's accident, our chain saw apprentice attacked the wood again. He and the axe men, also now more careful, spent hours hacking and chopping before finally bringing down the porch supports.

The old logs also took their toll on our troops. Aerin McQuiggen, an intelligent, stunningly beautiful blonde, was an incredibly hardworking woman. She holds down a full-time job as a waitress, while carrying a full load at school and keeping up a high grade-point average. It had not occurred to me to suggest that the students wear long blue jeans. Shorts are the standard uniform in Texas during the summer.

Aerin was wearing a pair of very short shorts. She and one of the boys picked up a long porch beam and started toward the trash trailer with it. Suddenly, the old, decaying log broke at the end Aerin was carrying, leaving a long, jagged point of wood. As it fell, the point scraped along the front of her leg. We were fortunate, once again, that it was just a scratch. But it meant one more wounded warrior for Lynette. Aerin took her wound better than either David or Brian, stopping only long enough for Lynette to clean and bandage her leg before getting back to work.

Inside the cabin, the thick piles of dried mature and hay had to be removed. Susan Locklear and Thomas Vanderberg from the graduate class were joined by Gabby Whitlock, Jason Surmiller, Mark Johnson, Cory Stanford, and Michael Blackwell from the undergraduate class, attacked sixty years of accumulated manure and hay. Dust billowed up in the enclosed cabin. The students emerged choking and coughing, tears streaming from their eyes. Shawn raced to town for masks and goggles. Thus protected, Susan again led her team into the interior. The hay and manure had solidified over the years. The shovels made little impact. The piles could only be broken up with heavy rakes, although pickaxes would have worked better.

Slowly, the piles of manure outside grew and the floorboards inside were soon swept clean. At last, Susan emerged with her racoon-faced troops. Their eyes and mouths, covered by the goggles and masks, remained white while their faces were streaked with muddy sweat, their clothing covered with brown dust. One of the girls insisted on keeping several large garbage bags of manure for her garden. Even I got involved in the digging and found a perfect, round cow patty, which covered with shiny shellac, made a great award for the best student.

Meanwhile the gentlemanly Dr. Lovell had taken it upon himself to provide us with latrine facilities. He said he had been in the military and knew how to make a latrine. Just dig a three- or four-foot-deep hole with a wooden bench over the top with a hole cut in it. Properly gotten up in an Australian campaign hat, a neat, blue polo shirt and neatly pressed jeans, he set off into the woods with a shovel, an axe, a blue tarp, some yellow rope and several rolls of toilet paper. He headed for a small grove of trees down the hill from the cabin. Several hours later, with the heat of the afternoon bearing down on all of us, he reemerged. Dripping with sweat, his hat crumpled, his coveralls stained and muddy, blisters on both hands that once again called for the efforts of Lynette, our EMT.

The latrine was neatly surrounded by the blue tarp, the rolls of toilet paper hung on the yellow cord, and a white flag placed at the edge of the woods to indicate "In Use." The three-foot deep hole, however, had dwindled to a mere three inches. The roots of the surrounding trees had defeated his best intentions. He left the shovel for end-users to simply scoop dirt over whatever was necessary. As it turned out, the heat was so intense, and the students' efforts so great, that everyone sweated out any liquid that might have made the latrine necessary. But we had it if we needed it.

The intrepid eighty-four-year-old Laura Johnston also showed up at the cabin ready to help. The Good Lord had been with us so far, but I was not taking any more chances. She helped with the food and water, but I turned her around and sent her back to town to work on her report.

By Friday, we had removed most of the porches. Only the roof remained, along with huge piles of scrap lumber. In Texas, ranchers often fill erosion-prone gullies with trash to lessen the effect of "gully-washing" runoffs. We needed a long trailer to haul the scraps to the creek edge where Keefer wanted us to dump the wood. The SHSU Physical Plant loaned us a sixteen-foot trailer, and several of the students appointed themselves the "dumping crew." All the boards that could be saved were laid aside, but everything else was loaded onto the trailer. The students went bumping off across the pasture, laughing uproariously over who-knows-what as they disappeared over the hill.

We met Maggie Farris Parker for the first time on Friday. The owner and donor of the cabin was delicate and ladylike, carefully made up, elegantly coiffed and not looking anywhere near her age. Without hesitation, she jumped right in. She began pulling nails out of the wood we had saved for the rebuilding of the cabin. She separated the ancient, rusting license plates and stacked then as mementos. She carried the wood scraps to the trailer right along with the students. Her make-up disappeared onto her sleeves as she wiped off the sweat streaming down her face. Her hat ruined her elegant hairdo, but she kept at it. Her humor was infectious, and when she banged her thumb with a hammer, she didn't even go to Lynette for help. We decided that she was definitely one of the team.

The roof was a challenge. Fearing the midday heat on Thursday, I had put off doing the roof until Friday morning when it was cooler. The pitch of the roof was steep, the tin slippery, and even at eight a.m., the heat and humidity were already increasing rapidly. Several of the young men faced a paralyzing fear of heights and climbed to the thirty-foot peak. Reagan Greer, Bryan Rogers, Chris Ortiz, and Alex St. Peter, clambered up the long ladders, crowbars in hand. Fearing tumbling off backwards, they used the pry bars to pull the nails from the corrugated tin roof, clinging for dear life as the pressure of their efforts tipped them backwards. Don Fink, a kindly, powerful giant of a man and ex-Marine came up with our motto. "We ain't skeered." From then on, no matter what we had to do, we weren't "skeered."

Maxia and I were worried about how to keep the boys from slipping off the roof. We tied them on with safety ropes and jury-rigged ladders anchored to pickups on the far side of the cabin. The young men found that the ladders and the ropes got in the way and soon pitched our ropes and fears off the roof. They sat or crawled across the tin, using only the traction from their rubber-soled sneakers to keep them from falling off.

As the sun rose, they pried up the nails and peeled off the tin, one sheet at a time. It was an excruciatingly hot, slow process but they refused to quit. It may have become a point of honor to finish stripping the roof. Lynette badgered then to come down for water breaks. When they refused, she began throwing bottles of Gatorade and ammonia-soaked washcloths up to them. At least they had to stop to rest while they drank and wrapped the wet cloths around their heads and around their necks. The rest of us stayed out of the way as they slid the heavy sheets off the roof. Then we would hurry back in to collect the scraps and load up another trailer load to take to the gullies.

Once the tin was removed, we had to remove the long thin strips of lath nailed to the rafters. Three of us climbed up the thin lath, using it like a ladder. We could look down through the empty space to see the floor of the cabin floor—thirty feet of *empty space* below us. Since the lath was thin and cracked easily under our weight, we had to keep our feet close to the large rafters for support. Working together on each lath, the three of us inserted prybars and pulled off each strip along the length of the roof, one piece at a time. We had to be careful not to pull too hard or we could fall over backwards and roll off the roof. Maxia decided we were taking way too much time.

As the sun crept toward noon and the heat intensified, Maxia and I met for a conference. We were both worried about whether we would finish. He was impatient with the slow, laborious process. With the lath and tin removed from one side of the roof, and part of the tin removed from the second side, we found that most of the rafters had deteriorated from dry rot and termites. They would be unusable. At that point, he decided we should just rip the roof off. Time was becoming critical. I worried about the damage to the cabin itself if the rafters crashed down on the cabin.

Maxia chose the spots where we were to attach the ropes to the rafters. All thirty students took hold of the ropes and pulled. Nothing happened. Shawn, who had arrived with more supplies, clambered up on the roof. No one could tell clearly what was still holding the roof up. We passed him a sledgehammer, and he began pounding om the rafters, not realizing they were the very ones he was standing on. Suddenly, with one last blow, the rafters broke free. The beam on which was standing collapsed, and Shawn disappeared into the roof.

Not knowing whether to laugh or call for an ambulance, we rushed inside to find him hanging from one of the rafters that he had caught hold of on his way down. He let go and fell the last few feet to the floor, bouncing up again as if nothing had happened. Being the good sport he is, joined in the laughter at his gymnastics. He had, however, scratched his back so Lynette had another wounded warrior to tape up. She cleaned and dressed his scrapes and he was back pulling on the rope in no time. "I ain't skeert."

Determined to get the roof off, Maxia finally attached the ropes to his pickup truck. With the truck and all the students pulling, the rafters finally gave way with a creaking groan. I winced as the roof came crashing down on the cabin. The inter-locked logs of the cabin didn't move. Now all we had to do was haul off the rotten rafters, the splintered lath, and the sheets of tin. The cabin was almost ready to be moved by Howard Long the next day. Several of the students, including Aerin, Alex, Roberto, Don and Chris, remained until nearly dark to finish cleaning up the site.

By Saturday morning, the little cabin, eighteen feet by eighteen feet, looking tiny and forlorn, was sitting on the hill. The pessimists among us were sure the cabin would not withstand the trip into town. The lower beams were weak with dry rot and termites. The fireplace wall was still sagging, the logs blackened and charred. Some of the points of the half dovetail joints had broken off over the years. The interlocking corners, although they looked sturdy, could easily come apart. The doorjambs, to which the logs were nailed, would keep the logs in place as long as the nails held. Shawn and I (the optimists among us) were hopeful that it could withstand anything.

Shawn and I got to the site early. As Howard Long had ordered, we had brought sheets of plywood to nail over the cabin logs to hold them in place. There was one lone tree along the pasture road and one of its branches extended over the road. I told Shawn we needed to cut off the branch in order to get the cabin out.

He and I loaded up a ladder and saw and drove down to the offending tree. I leaned the ladder against the bole of the small tree and climbed up to cut off the limb. Ladders, as a rule, have horizontal, flat rungs, and trees are round. This was, evidently, not a concept which I had clearly grasped. As I reached up for the limb with one hand and the saw in the other, the top of the ladder suddenly slid around the trunk of the tree, twisting out from under me.

I managed to hang onto the limb with one hand and promptly dropped the saw. I grabbed the branch and hung there like a very large, uncomfortable monkey. There I dangled, a dozen feet in the air, my legs thrashing as I struggled to reach the ladder. My fright turned to hysterical laughter. The ever-gallant Shawn came running to my rescue, by this time laughing as hard as I was. He grabbed me around the legs trying to hold me up. I knew I couldn't let go, sure I would fall on him and squash him flat.

Through peals of laughter, I told him to get the ladder. Just at this juncture, stone-faced Howard Long and two of his workers drove up. They just sat in their trucks, staring at us. Shawn finally got the ladder under me again and helped me down, both of us gasping with laughter, as much at the picture we must have presented as the deadpan silence with which Howard and his men greeted us.

We had not accomplished our mission of cutting off the limb. It turned out that was the least of our worries. Howard was not happy with the state of the cabin. We had not nailed on the plywood, and the sixteen-foot two-by fours which Shawn had also bought at great expense, had not been nailed across the top of the cabin to brace the logs. Several of the students showed up and we began nailing on the plywood. Since I knew we would have to take the plywood off eventually, I was nailing sparingly.

Evidently our tap-tap-tapping was not at all what Howard had in mind. He ordered one of his workers to get out the pneumatic nail gun. Before we knew it, they were emptying hundreds of rounds of nails into the plywood and the logs. That plywood wasn't ever coming off, but then again, the logs weren't going to move either. It was like putting a wooden corset on our cabin.

For the next several hours, Howard and his men worked to insert two giant steel I-beams under the cabin. For our part, Maxia, Shawn, our student helpers, and I, dug out more manure from under the cabin. We cleared porch supports, moved rocks from under the cabin and got the heck out of the way. Howard was not used to civilian help.

Howard was worried. The I-beams had been run under the cabin about a third of the way in from either side. Since there were no floor joists underneath the cabin, the I-beams were in contact with only the two lowest logs of the front and back wall stacks. Howard chained the steel beams to the two bottom logs of the cabin. The entire weight of the cabin—several tons of logs—rested only on those two bottom floor joists. The logs looked sturdy, but there were signs of internal dry rot and termite damage. There was nothing to keep the sides from collapsing if either of those beams gave way.

By two p.m. on Saturday afternoon, the cabin was chained onto the I-beams. Howard's crew had attached the massive dual tires, one set to the back end of each I-beam. He had hooked chains around the front end of the beams, and they hung from the hoist of a very large tow truck. We were only two hours behind schedule.

A small audience had formed. Maxia, Keefer, Maggie, Shawn and I had been joined by the neighbors, Robert "Bob" and Toni Bruner who were lending moral support. With us also was Walker County Constable John Hook.

A week before the move, I had called Howard to make sure everything was in order. He asked if we had gotten the permits.

Permits? What permits?

It seemed that moving an oversized load on state highways requires a permit from the Texas Department of Transportation, signed by everyone from the governor on down. These permits normally take six weeks to process. We had a week.

I hurried down to the local TxDOT office and asked for the form. They gave it to me with a shake of their heads at the unlikely possibility that we could get a permit in time. I handed the form off to Shawn, ever the efficient bureaucrat. Shawn got the city to waive the one hundred dollar fee then he started on the rounds of the many offices involved.

He secured signatures from county officials, city officials, the county sheriff's office, the city police, the phone company (we are still not sure why they needed to see the permit), the power company—in case overhead lines needed to be moved—and, of course, the TxDot offices. In addition, he had to get permission from the TxDOT construction crews who were working on a three-year project to widen the main bridge into town. The workers would have to move their barricades and construction equipment for us to bring the cabin through.

By good fortune, since it was not a "house" by the usual definition of the term, and since it was under twenty feet, we did not need to send the form to Austin for the governor's signature. Shawn convinced the lady at the TxDOT office to call the request in. Austin insisted on the make and model of Howard's truck and the license plate numbers of the truck and trailer.

Thank goodness for cell phones. Shawn called me. I called Howard. He called his wife. She checked the trailer which was at their home. By Friday we had the permit with all the signatures.

At two p.m. the next day, with the cabin sitting precariously on its I-beams and the truck thundering to life, Howard asked for the permit. It was nowhere to be found. Shawn knew he had it somewhere, completed with all the signatures, but he could not find it. I assured Howard that everything really was in order.

Stoically, Howard shrugged. This was, after all, East Texas. When Constable Hook drove up, we learned that he was Howard's cousin. The two men shook hands, slapped each other on the back, gossiped about family, and no permit was ever mentioned. Shawn and I found the permit several days later in a stack of papers at the Main Street office.

Slowly, Howard's huge truck started off down the hill. The cabin rocked along behind. The dirt road was narrow and the big dual tires, attached to each of the I-beams, extended sixteen feet, edge-to-edge, well beyond the sides of the dirt track. Several times, Howard had to detour out into the pasture to avoid having the tires drop off the track into the ditches cut alongside the road. The cabin swayed as he rolled over the drainage ditches, but it was holding together.

As we approached the entrance to the pasture, the small parade came to a stand-still. The cabin was eighteen feet wide. The pasture gate only had a sixteen-foot opening. Bob Bruner went running for his tractor and a chain saw. He and Maxia pulled out the steel gate supports on both sides and, ever so slowly, Howard crept through.

Past the gate, the road narrowed as it passed under decorative trees and vegetation around the house. The house belonged to the Farris family, but it was rented by an elderly couple. The couple watched in horror as Maxia and Bob chain-sawed several trees which were in the way, dropping them crashing into the forest beyond the house.

One of the side logs under the cabin suddenly caught on a thick vine. The cabin started to shift sideways. Everyone yelled to stop the truck. Howard leaped down from the truck. He worked his way back through the underbrush, now clinging thickly to the side of the cabin, to survey the problem.

Bruner and Maxia, sweating in the heat, cut the vine and all the men pulled the cabin back into place with cables and come-alongs. Cautiously, Howard climbed back in the cab and started up again. The road curved close to the house, and the roof extended out into the path of the truck. With only inches to spare, the cabin slid past the corner of the house.

County roads in Texas are often built with deep ditches on either side for water run-off during the spring rains. At the entrance to each property, narrow bridges of hard-packed dirt, wide enough for cars, are built over large culverts or pipes. There is no edge or curb to keep residents from going off into the ditch. It is up to the property owner to mark the edges of the narrow road as they see fit.

The width of the entry road over the culvert was fourteen feet. The ditch on either side of the road was six feet deep. Howard's dual tires measured sixteen feet outside-to-outside. Inside- to-inside, the tires measured thirteen feet. This gave him six inches on each side, about half the width of the inner tires for traction. If the inside tires held, the outside tires would hang, unsupported, over the six-foot-deep culvert.

Slowly, with a man positioned along each fender to guide him, Howard started across the culvert. The two outside tires sagged as the road disappeared from beneath them. The inside tires tilted as they tried to follow their partners into empty space. The I-beams, to which the tires were attached, twisted and screeched. Once he was rolling, Howard did not stop. Dirt crumbled from the edges of the bridge and fell into the deep ditch under the pressure of the rolling tires. The tires held. Slowly, the massive load stabilized as the outside tires rolled up onto firm ground on the far side of the ditch. Everyone let out a gasp and began cheering, breathing again. Howard never changed expression.

CHAPTER 3

Rebuilding

Problems on the town square began at once. Stuart Cox, who arrived soon after we did, informed us in no uncertain terms that the cabin was facing the wrong way. The fireplace should face the side, not the back. The cabin would have to be turned.

Howard insisted that Maxia had told him which was the front, and who should know better than the owner? He wasn't moving the cabin because there wasn't room enough to maneuver the big truck between the cabin and the walls of the adjacent buildings. Stuart insisted. Howard walked off, never to be seen again. Shawn and I looked at each other. At lease we had a cabin, and it was safely on the town square.

On Monday morning, I set up the canopies, coolers, tables, chairs, tools, and supplies in front of the cabin. The students would be coming in smaller groups this time, except at class time. The purpose now was to dry-in the cabin, pull out all the floorboards, repair or replace the floor joists, and fix the logs we could. The cabin, however, was still up on the I-beams.

We started with the floor. Stuart had suggested that we stabilize the cabin by using steel cables looped around the logs and connected from side to side. Then we could build scaffolding across the top of the cabin. With the cables in place, we thought we were safe enough to pull up the floorboards that were nailed across the floor joists. Several students began tearing out floorboards. Others, meanwhile, using Keefer's trailer, removed all the nails and hauled the boards to Maxia's car wash. They scrubbed off years of dirt and grime with brushes and towels. They brought back the clean boards and stacked them against the wall of the building next door, ready to be reused.

The larger, thick floor joists were hollowed out with years of dry rot. We used the chainsaw (Darren Jones had become quite adept at handling it) to notch one of the logs whose end was beyond fixing. Bob Bruner, the neighbor, had given us old hewn logs from a very similar building he had torn down. We used one of the short pieces to splice it onto the floor joist and glued the wood pieces together. The rest of the joists, we hoped, could be salvaged with enough filler and glue.

Mac Woodward was still resisting getting roped into working on the cabin. He was losing the battle. Still quietly shaking his head, he provided us with enough epoxy resin to fill the holes in the floor joists. To make the very expensive resin stretch further, we mixed it with fine cedar shavings donated by Doug Winters, the owner of the beautiful cedar furniture store. From the Woods store, right around the corner, Ann Porter and Susan Gutierrez, assisted by Alex and Ross Lovell, stirred and mixed the gloppy mess and filled the long, jagged holes in the tops of the logs. The epoxy hardly made a dent.

While one team was filling and mixing, a second group turned our attention to the roof. To be historically accurate we would need to use "shakes" or "shingles." Shakes are narrow pieces of wood, usually about twenty-four inches long, and eight to fifteen inches wide. They are split off large logs of white or yellow oak, cedar or cypress. A shingle is a shake which has been planed down with a drawknife so that it has a thinner edge at one end to fit under the shingles above it.

Pat Nolan had given us a contact at the Woodville Heritage Village and Museum for someone who could teach us how to make the shakes. I called and made an appointment for Mr. David Rust to drive down from Woodville to give us a demonstration. A tall, stooped, quiet, elderly man, he arrived with his tools. He had a froe, an oak mallet, a small bench and a square support to hold the log. By good fortune, Keefer had given us some cedar logs, each about eighteen inches in diameter and two feet tall. We appropriated one for our shake lesson.

A froe is an eighteen-inch-long steel blade with a sharp edge along its bottom side. At one end, it has a round handle pointing up, to hold the blade in place against the top of the large log. Mr. Rust squared off the cedar block by cutting off the outer edges of the log, both the bark and the fast-growing cambium layer.

Holding the squared-off log in the wooden support with his feet, he sat on the bench and placed the blade of the froe on the log, about an inch from the edge. He held the upright handle with his left hand and with his right, he brought down the heavy oak mallet on the back of the blade. Like magic, the wood split cleanly all the way to the bottom of the log. A shake fell off. It looked so easy.

It seems that splitting shingles and using froes is something like playing championship golf. It looks so simple when the pros do it. We had ordered two froes (the only two left in existence, it seemed) from our friends at Walker County Ace Hardware.

Alex took one of the froes and the oak mallet and sat down on the bench in front of the log. He placed the froe exactly the way Mr. Rust had done it—or so we thought. When he whacked down on the froe, nothing happened. He heaved up and whacked it again. The froe entered about an inch and stuck fast.

While we all stood around in awe, he hammered on the part of the froe still sticking out beyond the edge of the log. After multiple tries, he finally forced the froe through the wood. A rickety-looking shake peeled off. He gladly handed the froe to the next candidate.

As each of the rest of us took our turn, we found that splitting shakes is a daunting task. By the time a dozen of us had finished trying the technique, we were covered with sweat and worn out. We had a stack of twelve shakes. Mr. Rust nodded and said, "Now, you only need about two thousand more." A tin roof suddenly sounded much more plausible. I sent a team running back to the gullies to retrieve as much of the tin from the roof as they could scavenge.

We also needed trusses for our roof. I spray-painted a triangular form on the concrete parking lot behind the cabin. The truss would be eighteen feel long at the base, four feet high at the peak, with a three-foot overhang on each end. The ground crew, made up of whoever could hold a hammer (which meant most of the class, by now) pulled the rafters out of the stack we had brought from the site. Some of the beams were rotten, but we cut the good ones at an angle and laid them out on our form. We nailed the points of the rafters together at the peak, strengthening them by crossing them with two-by-fours. We stacked them against the wall waiting to put them up on the roof. I figured they would work fine just to get a roof up. I was wrong.

Stuart Cox arrived in all his busy, bustling German efficiency. Trusses, he said, were not historic. It made no difference to him that they were temporary. He insisted we put up a ridgepole down the length of the building.

Stuart appropriated two of the four-by-six oak beams that Bob Bruner had given us. Back we went to Doug Winters. He notched and spliced the two boards so they now formed a twenty- two-foot ridgepole. Under Stuart's direction, we put up supports at each end of the roof and mounted the ridgepole.

In writing about putting up a ridgepole, it sounds like a very simple task. It wasn't. We were working standing on rickety ladders, balancing along the top of the walls and climbing across from side to side on two-by-four scaffolding. The end supports were heavy and unwieldy, the ridgepole was massive, and the effort to nail in the four-inch-long spikes took all the energy we could muster.

We were all dizzy with the exertion, dripping with sweat, and gasping for breath as we strained to hold the heavy wood while the nailing crew secured them in place. Finally, the ridgepole was up, and it was solid. We were all getting a clear understanding of why raising a barn required the work of an entire community.

A courageous student roofing crew had formed, made up of big Don Fink, Sadaqat Amin, Reagan Greer, Aerin McQuiggen, and

Chris Ortiz. Others joined in as they showed up at odd intervals. The only requirement was not being "skeert" of heights. The dedicated team swallowed their fear and clambered up to work on the wobbly scaffolding. Stuart tore apart all of our triangular trusses. We recut the rafters to extend from the ridgepole to the edge of the cabin. The roofing team balanced along the top logs and stood on the scaffolding to hold the rafters in place while the others nailed. Because the scaffolding didn't reach across the entire top of the cabin, they had to stand or cling at difficult angles to reach around the ridgepole in order to nail the rafters into place. The hammers were heavy, the nails long and hard to drive. When one team member wore out, shoulders aching, arms throbbing, and hands blistered, the next one stepped in. No one ever gave up, and no one complained. They remained cheerful throughout. I was amazed, and so very proud of these courageous, dedicated, determined young people.

We had one week left to finish up the cabin for the dedication ceremony on August 3rd. While the glue team finished the floor joists, we concentrated on getting the cabin dried-in and the roof finished. Keefer had helped me, and he had taken the tin to be cut into smaller sections. One roof team attached one-by-two lath across the rafters. Then we began nailing on the tin.

Like so many other tasks we had faced, nailing tin is another one of those jobs that is much harder than it looks. If we didn't get the point of the nail through the tin on the first shot, it merely bounced off, usually right out of our fingers. If we really smacked the nail hard enough to go into the tin, we invariably whacked our fingers along with the nail.

The roofing team dismissed fear and accepted the fact that bruised and battered fingers would be our constant companions. Out of desperation, one of the boys (Chris Ortiz, I think), invented a nail holder. He cut a narrow slit in a piece of one-by-two. The nail slid into the slot and would be held steady until we hit it with the hammer. His fingers stayed safely out of the way. We all copied his invention.

It rarely rains in July or August, and we had hoped to have the roof completed before any chance showers came our way. Our luck had run out, however, and the rains came. We were almost three-quarters done. Desperate to finish the roof, our roofing crew continued working. Aerin and Chris nailed on one side while Don Fink and I nailed on the opposite side. Sadaqat passed the tin up to us.

To nail the tin along the edges, we had to lie spread-eagle across the tin, balancing on one toe on the thin lath, stretching to hold the nails, and hammering as best we could. The rain dripped from our noses and our matted hair, our clothes drenched and grimy from lying on the tin, our arms and legs streaked with sweat and mud. As we looked at each other, we couldn't help bursting into laughter.

We were a ludicrous-looking bunch. We were laughing so hard we were in tears but we had not quite finished nailing on the tin. The little cabin had been rained on before and it would certainly not melt. I finally called off the work for the day, and we all climbed down, dripping and still laughing. We had one day to finish.

The following day, I sent Sadaqat and several of the future coaches to finish the roof. I stayed at the office with Susan Locklear and some of the female students to finish the programs and get the awards ready for the ceremony.

Suddenly, one of the students came running in. Sadaqat was on the phone. The corner of the cabin, where the fireplace had left the logs unsupported, had collapsed. Two of the boys had been on the roof. I grabbed the phone. Were the students all right? He assured me they were frightened but had not been hurt since the roof had held. I raced down to the cabin site.

The two young men (Chris Lincecum and Rick Herndon, if my memory serves) were still shaking. They had been nailing on the last few strips of tin when they heard a snap. The roof began to tilt. With a jolt, the roof stopped listing and they scrambled for the ladders and the safety of the ground. The back support log, which had been sitting on the I-beam had finally broken.

The steel cables, unable to hold the logs together, had snapped. The dovetail joints on the back corner of the cabin had given way. The only thing that kept the logs from falling off the I-beams, and probably bringing the whole structure down, was Susan Locklear's ice chest. Still supporting the logs, it lay, partially crushed, under the corner of the cabin.

I called off the roofing. It was already almost three in the afternoon. How could we fix the cabin before the dedication ceremony at ten the next morning? Both university and city officials had been invited, as well as dozens of friends of the Farris and Roberts families.

In desperation, I called Mac at the museum. He arrived and discussed the situation with Bob Bruner who had also arrived. Bob suggested Joe Soliz of Ace Foundation Repair and House Leveling. I called and begged for his help.

Joe appeared within the hour. He and Mac and Bob inspected the logs. Joe shook his head. There was nothing he could do that evening, since his crews were all tied up on other jobs. He would be there at seven in the morning.

I returned to the office to finish the last of the awards. To my relieved delight, Susan and the students had already put the finishing touches on them. There was nothing more any of us could do.

The next morning, while we were preparing for the ceremony out front, Joe Soliz and his men worked in the back. They jacked up the cabin, clamped steel struts under the broken beam and pulled the corner back into alignment. Stuart, Maxia, Keefer, Bob and Mac, and practically every other man in the crowd gathered around. They all offered opinions and suggestions.

Joe Soliz, a thorough professional, smiled politely and ignored the advice. He had more help than he could use with all the heads poking in and around the collapsed corner. He finished on time and I paid him with the last of our university money, just as Shawn made the introductory comments out front.

We had asked Reverend Roger Shuemate from the original Farris Chapel out at West Sandy to give the invocation. James Patton welcomed the large crowd and provided the historical background. There were descendants from both the Farris clan and the Roberts family. Lucille Farris Benthal, a descendant of both families, provided posters of the family genealogy. Four generations of the Roberts family attended, including the well-known Huntsville luminary, Poncho Roberts. With him were his wife Sugar, their son, grandson and his ninety-three-year-old aunt, Sally Sandford Roberts Zulch.

Ernest Brown attended and told us he had honeymooned in the cabin with his wife in 1939. He was pleased to meet the students and tell them stories of living in the cabin as a tenant farmer. Their lives had been much like the stories told by Mary Blankenship except for the lack of natives.

The crowd also consisted of friends of the families, university officials and city administrators. At the back of the crowd stood the Texas History students, graduates and undergraduates, modest at all the praise but proudly resplendent in Cabin Fever T-shirts.

Maggie Farris Parker read a moving address. She and her brothers dedicated the cabin to the city of Huntsville and the people of Walker County. Carol Williams of the Frameworks Gallery had put together a large frame containing one of the 1933 license plates. In addition, it contained a wonderful picture of the cabin by Susan Locklear, as it had been in the pasture with the trumpet vine cascading over the roof. We presented the picture to the Farris family.

Susan and I then handed out the "special worker" awards. Our staunch supporters, Maxia and Keefer Farris, Stuart Cox and Mac Woodward, received yellow hard hats decorated with their names, and covered in chips of wood, and old rusty nails from the cabin. We gave Maggie the Purple Thumb Award, a large, well-worn work glove with the thumb painted an appropriate red.

During our work downtown, Susan Locklear had brought her young neighbor, Ashleigh to help. Don Fink and David Parnell had brought their daughters, Courtney Fink and Fallon Parnell, to help at the cabin. All three young ladies were honored with princess crowns and toy hammers decorated with glitter for their work.

The Save Our Souls Sustenance Award went to Rick Erck and Sarah Hall who had kept us so well fed. Our motherly Lynnette Nadeau received the Florence Nightingale Award.

The remainder of the awards went to the working crews. The Wrecking Crew Awards (work gloves glued around large plastic tools) belonged to Melinda Bonnert, Rodney Ross, John Turner, and Jeff Nutt. Recipients of the Clean Cabin Cow Patty Awards (glitter-covered masks and goggles) were Susan Locklear, Michael Blackwell, Jason Surmiller, Mark Johnson, and Thomas Vanderberg. The Tough Texas Women (Powderpuff dolls glued onto the 1933 license plates) were Gabby Whitlock, Miranda Hubbard, and Melissa Bridges.

The Testosterone Crew (Wrestler Mania dolls attached to orange shields) were Chris Lincecum, Cory Stanford, Nathan Davis and Bryan Rogers. We gave Alex St. Peter a special Testosterone Award for his efforts with the axe against the *bois d'arc* tree. The Black and Blue Purple Heart Awards (purple hearts taped over with decorated bandages in gold frames) were, of course given to David Parnell, Brian Peterson, Rick Herndon and Shawn Lewis. Darren Jones and David Parnell received the Chain Saw Awards (small saws on a gold chain). The Glue Crew Wards (bottles of Elmer's glue on white ribbons) went to Ann Porter and Susan Gutierrez.

Our final awards were particularly heartfelt. We had to explain the Outhouse Award (a golden cord with a roll of toilet paper on it) when we gave it to Dr. Ross Lovell. For their extraordinary effort on the cabin roof and their work after hours, I awarded the Silver Star Awards to Sadaqat Amin, Chris Ortiz, Roberto Fernandez, and Reagan Greer.

By this time, Aerin McQuiggin must have decided she had been forgotten. Not so. For her and Don Fink, however, I had reserved the Medal of Honor Awards—large silver platters mounted with Texas flags and nails from the cabin. Their cheerful good humor and their willingness to work at whatever had to be done had made the whole project wonderful for all of us.

Susan and Lynette concluded the awards by giving me a miniature wooden cabin, appropriately decorated with old nails, bits of hay, and pieces of cow manure. James Patton closed the ceremony and Reverend Shuemate gave the benediction.

As we left the little cabin, sitting crookedly on its I-beams, we knew there had to be more to come. The students were depressed at having to leave it unfinished. They had become totally committed to the cabin. It was, and always would be, their cabin. Their sweat, blood, and even a few tears had baptized it.

Sadaqat Amin had brought his video camera to the site during the days of the move. He had been able to capture some of the work. At our last class, Sadaqat videotaped interviews with several of us. He put together a video that included shots of the cabin and the students during the demolition and the rebuilding. He played it for us on the last day of class.

The semester was over. It had indeed been a class that none of us would ever forget. But the cabin was unfinished and I had no Texas History classes in the Fall semester. How could we save the cabin?

CHAPTER 4

Renovation

The little cabin was sitting smack in the middle of Shawn's Main Street Project. None of us could ignore it for long. All of the Main Street Board members supported the project, but there was neither money nor a long-term labor force.

We failed to find Howard, who was moving a house somewhere near Navasota. It was evident he was not going to turn the cabin for us. The only way we could get the cabin off the I-beams was to disassemble the logs. It broke my heart, but all our hard work in reroofing the cabin would have to be undone. If we could stack the logs, perhaps in the spring I would have another Texas History class who could help with the rebuilding.

The new semester had started. Before school really gets rolling there are always student groups willing to volunteer for projects. A wonderful colleague of mine, Robert "Ty" Cashion, had just become the sponsor for an "animal house" fraternity, the Delta Nu chapter of Sigma Tau Gamma. Ty is a congenial, slightly balding redhead, given to practical jokes. He taught U.S. and Western history, but he is probably most famous for his book, *Pigskin Pulpit*. Ty was still new at SHSU and would have a hard time refusing a request from a senior colleague.

Ty had been working hard to get his fraternity men to focus on something other than booze, brawling, and broads. He was searching for a project that the boys could work on. It had to be no more than a few days, and which would give them some good publicity, rather than the usual notoriety.

I told Ty we needed about a dozen strong men to help dismantle the cabin. I would offer hamburgers, pizza, and Cokes afterwards. He jumped at the chance for his guys to look good. It took some encouragement and pep talks, but the boys agreed to take on the task of dismantling the cabin. The attraction of ripping and tearing was always effective.

During the following week, Shawn and I prepared the site for the demolition. We bought two-by-fours to build "cradles" to hold the logs off the ground. They were nailed together into square frames, eight feet by eight feet, then attached to twelve-inch legs at the corners and at several points in between. I had four frames, one for the logs for each wall of the cabin.

Once again, I was a little unclear on the concept. I had misjudged both the weight and size of the logs. I wouldn't find out my error for a few more weeks. We spray-painted letters and numbers on each log for the sides of the walls and one through sixteen for the logs themselves.

Again, I made several mistakes. It would take massive amounts of scrubbing to get the paint off when we reassembled the cabin. The letters did not correspond with the way we eventually wanted the cabin to sit. For those kind readers planning to reassemble cabins, try using small letters and numbers on cards, tacked onto the logs. Also, make sure those reassembling know what is meant by "left" and "right." It made a big difference.

The following Saturday, Ty showed up with his fraternity. They were startled when they arrived on the site and realized the chore facing them. Gamely, they approached the cabin as a challenge to their masculinity. It was a good opportunity to show off their muscles.

I had brought out the hammers and prybars which we had used only a few weeks earlier to build the roof. The guys climbed up and began hammering off the tin. I could scarcely bear to watch, but it was necessary surgery.

When they attacked the rafters, the lath and the ridgepole, I felt a hidden sense of satisfaction (through the tears) that they really had to work hard to knock our rafters loose. The ridgepole and supports gave way even more grudgingly as the four-inch nails pulled out. Finally, the cabin was back to just the four log walls.

I had seen pictures of Carroll and Mae Tharpe disassembling their cabins. Since logs were not nailed, but merely stacked, connected by the dove tailed joints at the corners, we thought it would be easy. The pictures I had seen suggested it was. Carroll and Mae had secured each log with ropes. Then, working from the top on the two side walls, they slid the logs down sloping poles to the ground. Simple.

It was not as neat as the pictures had led me to believe. I had the fraternity men lean the leftover rafters against the cabin. Looping the nylon rope over the logs, one on each end, they would lift the logs and slide them down the rafters. They had to lift the logs to keep from breaking the tips off the dovetail notches.

The logs turned out to be incredibly heavy. The rope slipped through the boys' gloves, which I had insisted they wear. When they wrapped the rope around their hands, the rope wouldn't give at all. They were almost pulled off the wall by the weight.

It took several logs before they got the hang of it. Lifting the logs, they lowered the logs by letting the rope play out slowly. Once a log was down, they had to switch walls, moving across the corners to the adjacent stack. There they repeated the process.

By the time they were within four logs of the ground, still some seven feet in the air, the wall should have been more stable. The logs at the bottom, however, were dry-rotted and termite-damaged. The dovetail joints were frail. One of the boys was up on the wall, switching corners, when the joints gave way. It was the same corner that had collapsed three weeks earlier.

This time, there was no ice chest to stop the fall. As the logs fell, the young man leaped for his life. He landed no more than a foot from the toppled logs. As the fright passed, we all broke into relieved laughter. Our hero staggered over to sit down, knees shaking. Not that I wasn't worried about our young man, but I hurried over to check the logs. They were also unharmed.

With the corner down, it was easier to life off the logs. The dozen muscular young men easily moved the last of the logs. Now the problem was the cradles. The charming little two-by-four frames had withstood the first log although the heavy log extended five feet on either end of the wooden crossmembers. By the time the men laid the second log on the cradle, the two-by-four supports groaned and gave way. The frame settled to the ground. The only advantage I could see was that at least the logs were up off the ground, if only by four inches instead of the twelve inches I had planned on.

The cradles were also not nearly wide enough. The massive logs from each wall took up far more than the eight feet we had allotted for them. Soon we had giant timbers filling all of the space around what had been the cabin. They certainly looked much bigger on the ground than they had when attached to each other. They were also cumbersome, and in the way.

The tenants of the two adjacent buildings, who had to walk from the back parking lot to their front doors, had to pick their way around the beams. We promised them it would not be long before we got them out of the way. By the time the Tau Sigs got done laying out the logs, it was too late to clean up the site. We all adjourned for a celebratory feast of hamburgers and drinks.

September was a hard month. Our little cabin had ceased to exist. I felt miserable and depressed when I had to drive through downtown. The cabin site was a mess. Broken boards were piled everywhere. The logs were more or less supported on what was left of the cradles. I was still looking for a work force at the university. Shawn was trying to get support from the city. Our hopes for restoring the cabin were fading but we could not give up.

By October, four members of Rotaract, the college division of Rotary International, volunteered to spend one afternoon cleaning up the site and straightening the logs. We stacked the wood, covered it with tarps, and shifted the big logs out of the way. We threw away wheelbarrow loads of broken boards and bent nails. The site looked much better.

Sometime, when we weren't looking, Howard Long came and got his I-beams. We may never know whether he was upset at our having torn down the cabin after all his effort to move it into town. Perhaps it was just his taciturn way.

We finally received good news. City Manager Bob Hart, after several visits by Shawn, agreed that the project needed to be continued. Since the university had contributed $5,000 to the project, he felt that the city should contribute as well. The city's October budget included $10,000 towards the completion of the cabin. The problem, then, was a work force. If we had to pay for workers, the project would skyrocket into the hundreds of thousands of dollars. No one was willing to pay for that. We needed more volunteer labor.

One of the members of the Main Street Board was Ed Owens, a tall, powerfully built, soft-spoken personable gentleman. At the time, he was Director of Operations for the Texas Department of Criminal Justice (TDCJ). Ed was a native of Huntsville, his mother a long-time and popular teacher. His wife, Reecie, was a political figure on the state level. Ed had worked his way to the top of TDCJ and was noted for his efficiency and sensible management style. He also had a delightful demeanor, a vast political savvy, and was known for his fairness and honesty. As one colleague of his put it, "He's just a darn nice guy." (Actually, he didn't say "darn.")

The State Legislature of Texas had provided that TDCJ inmates may offer assistance to community work projects that benefit the local townspeople. During 2001, however, the system was short-staffed and woefully lacking in enough supervisory officers to carry out any projects outside of the prison units.

Shawn Lewis, never willing to take no for an answer, asked Ed for help. With Ed's support, Shawn contacted the Region I Director about the possibility of getting a labor force. In exchange for a work crew of ten to fifteen inmates, Shawn offered to supply the wood, specialized tools, and food and refreshments for the men. He also offered Stuart, Mac, and me as volunteer supervisors to assist with the restoration.

His list of jobs included repairing the logs by injecting resin and creating the shingles to be split from wooden logs supplied by Shawn. Also, the work crews were to prepare the foundations, reassemble the cabin, install the floor and roof, remove concrete from the grounds and assist in landscaping the site. After several calls, TDCJ Region I Director Jimmy Alford at last agreed.

Sergeant Neil Smith and his crew arrived from the Eastham Unit in late October. Neil Smith stands an imposing six-foot-six in his gray-and-blue uniform and straw cowboy hat. He is broad-shouldered with rugged features, and the most cheerful smile in the world. He is a respected and well-liked City Councilman in the neighboring town of Trinity. As a native Texan, his Texas roots go back several generations. He had worked at the Eastham Unit for almost twenty years. His most important qualification, however, was his skill as a carpenter.

When Sergeant Smith and his men arrived at the cabin, no one had been advised of his coming. There was no one there to greet him. He stared hopelessly at the piles of logs, the stacks of old lumber, the jumbled strips of lath and broken rafters. What on earth had he gotten into? What was to be done with this mess?

He was ready load up his men and return to Eastham when Shawn arrived on the run from the Main Street office, a block away. Shawn assured him that there would be supervisors to direct the operation. Meanwhile, Shawn asked Neil to have his men start by breaking out the concrete parking lot where the cabin would sit. Neil grudgingly agreed.

Those first few weeks were stressful for everyone. The greatest difficulty in starting the project was not knowing what to do first. None of us had ever faced a disassembled cabin and we had no clear direction. What logs would we use? Could we use new logs? How authentic did we need to be? Could we be authentic if we were using new logs? Neil waited for instructions and his men waited with him. He was becoming exasperated at the inaction. Digging up the concrete was not going to help rebuilding the cabin.

Frantically, Shawn called me. I, in turn, called Mac. He arrived almost immediately. The first meeting between Mac and Neil should have been recorded for posterity. It didn't look like much, a simple handshake and a "How ya doing?" But it was a match made in heaven. These were two tall Texans, Neil happily gregarious, Mac quietly reserved. They bonded with a friendship that rivalled Damon and Pythias. The two men worked as one—Neil with is carpentry skills and Mac with his knowledge of log cabin restoration. Together, they would make miracles happen.

Despite Shawn's promise, none of us had planned to be on site to supervise the reconstruction of the cabin. During the Fall semester, I had a full schedule, teaching classes every day. I agreed to come every morning before class and help where I could. Stuart was too elderly to supervise the whole construction and his wife was not about to let him be away from home that much.

Pat Nolan, Mac's boss at the museum, agreed to relieve Mac of his duties at the museum, delegating the Curator of Collections duties to others. Mac was assigned to the cabin as Project Supervisor. Neil, as his partner, would provide the labor force and the structural knowledge. With these two Texans, the cabin would get done.

Shawn and I were relegated to being go-fers. That is a Texan term meaning one who spends all their waking hours going "fer" things. Shawn, ever mindful of the budget, spent hours on the phone pleading for contributions of logs, lumber, nails, wood filler, more logs, tools, gloves, hammers, more logs, sand to fill the site, bricks for a walkway, more logs, water and electric lines for the cabin, an air conditioner, and more logs. He got everything he wanted for little or nothing.

Meanwhile, Shawn and I supplied food. One of the benefits for the Eastham crew working on the cabin was the "free" world food which we supplied. Instead of their usual prison fare, they ate tastier food. They appreciated our efforts most of the time.

Early in the mornings, we would run by the doughnut shop. Shawn brought the doughnuts, a jug of milk, and a jug of orange juice. Being the extravagant sort, I, on the other hand, loaded up with doughnuts, both glazed and chocolate, kolaches, orange juice, chocolate milk and cups of coffee.

By lunch time, we supplied hamburgers or fried chicken. Early in the project, the men complained he was too stingy. When I brought more, Shawn reprimanded me for being ridiculously wasteful. We soon figured out the right amounts and the men stopped complaining.

Once the ground had been cleared, Mac and Neil put their heads together and laid out a plan of action. They realized that they would have to make the decisions since no one had more experience at building than they did. They were frequently offered "helpful" advice from a constant stream of hangers-on. They soon learned to nod and agree, then as soon as the "advisors" had left, they went back to their original plans.

Mac and Neil even made a token effort, out of pure southern politeness, I think, to ask my advice. Although I was frustrated at not being able to pick up a tool and jump in there to help with the rest of the inmates, I learned to keep my mouth shut and stay out of the way. . . and bring more doughnuts.

The stress disappeared as the two tall Texans began to rebuild the cabin. First, it was evident that we needed a foundation. Mac and Neil agreed that some kind of solid support, even if it were not historic, would have to be used to carry the weight of the logs. Bob Bruner offered to bring some of the rocks which had originally been used for the cabin. But there were not enough of them. They were also cumbersome and unwieldy.

Years earlier, Keefer had salvaged a number of large concrete blocks which had been used as supports for a building at the old lumber mill. Mac and Neil agreed that the blocks— twenty-four inches square, ten inches thick, and weighing several pounds each—would be perfect.

Stuart Cox disagreed. They were not historic. Mac and Neil argued that they would be hidden under the dirt and no one would ever know they were there. Grudgingly, Stuart agreed.

Once the blocks were accepted, we needed some way to level them. Huntsville Blueprint, just down the street, loaned us their transit and level. While the inmates dug out the big square holes, we set up the transit and began measuring the depth of each hole. Once more, here was a simple-looking job that became a nightmare. Digging a hole that is perfectly level across the bottom is not easy. Dirt, especially East Texas red clay, has a nasty habit of clumping and globbing into chunks that refuse to smooth out. Put the measuring rod on top of a clod, and the hole is too shallow. Place it between the clumps, and the hole is too deep.

Since I was running the transit (the only job I was permitted to do), I had to call for constant changes. Time after time, inmates laboriously dug out dirt, then added more to bring it up to level. Once the concrete blocks were dropped into place, the problem was compounded. "It's too shallow...no, now it's too deep." "Lift the block... fill underneath." "No, remove some of that...no add more in the other corner...no, the OTHER corner."

Patiently, the inmates dug and filled, emptied and filled again. At long last, the concrete blocks were in place. Actually, pretty close to being level. I was back to delivering doughnuts.

The greatest danger for a log cabin is termites tunneling up through wood supports. Cedar is one of the few woods that termites don't like. Once again, Keefer came to our rescue. He brought in nine almost perfectly matched cedar logs. Mac and Neil placed the logs on each of the concrete blocks. With a little shimming, we were level and ready for the logs.

While some of the Eastham crew had been digging the holes, Mac had brought filler from the museum to repair the logs. The material had to be mixed with just the right amount of water and coloring to match the logs. Even then it did not really look log-like. One of the inmates who had learned to use Bondo to repair cars in the past, quickly picked up the technique of using the filler to patch the ends of the logs.

Most of the logs had lost the points of their dovetails and they needed to be replaced. The inmates patched the logs, which had been laid out in numerical order on the four sides of the cabin and repaired the points as closely as possible to what they had been.

Mac had been frustrated with my numbering system. It took a while to finally figure out that the old front and back logs were actually the two sides. The broken fireplace wall would, as Stuart had insisted, face to the side, turning the front toward the street.

The lowest logs from the original cabin were useless. Three of the four main support logs, which would sit on the cedar blocks, would have to be replaced. Mac and Neil decided to use one of the 160-year-old hewn logs supplied by Bob Bruner. The others would be reconstructed from twenty-foot oak logs cut down to size, replicating the original as closely as possible. No one would ever see them, like the concrete support blocks. Most of the remaining logs could still be used. The logs in the burned fireplace wall were replaced with more of Bob's historic hewn logs.

Once the first set of four logs was in place, Mac and Neil debated about the flooring. Should they use inauthentic trusses to support the floor? Or replace the floor joists themselves? Did a historic building have to meet city codes, since it would be used for the public? How sturdy did the floor have to be?

The two men decided on new floor joists, but they used sturdy, treated modern four-by- eights instead of the original logs. Again, no one would ever see them, and it was better to have a safe floor. They notched the support logs and laid in the floor joists, using levels to keep them even.

By this time, Mac and Neil had given up any pretense at "just supervising." The enthusiasm and exhilaration of working with the old logs had captivated them both. Heads together, bent over the logs, they discussed, measured, marked, cut, notched and lifted the joists into place. Their shirttails hung out and their sleeves were grimy from wiping sweat from their faces. The inmates, and the rest of us who gathered to watch, were mere supporting cast for their craftsmanship.

The inmates, however, had found a job which no one but they could have accomplished—splitting shakes. The first log we brought in for the shakes was a weathered old giant yellow oak from Steeley Lumber that was about twenty-four feet long. Keefer mentioned having seen the log there so I went over and asked if they would donate it. They readily agreed and cut it into twenty-four-inch sections for us that they called "rounds."

Shawn and I went over to the lumber mill in an old, beat-up city pick-up truck and loaded the ten rounds to bring back to the cabin site. In my usual naïve fashion, I assumed that this log would be plenty for the roof shakes. I had no idea how many shakes can be made out of a log. We soon learned that it is not many.

My students' feeble attempts at shingle-making had produced twelve shakes. The Eastham crew broke up into two competing teams, one African American and the other Mexican American. The shakes were flying off the logs as the friendly competition escalated.

The teams started off using our brand-new, shiny, still-sharp froes. The oak mallet was soon abandoned in favor of sledgehammers. One inmate held the froe in place while the other hit it with the sledge. Once the blade of the froe was partially buried in the wood, they had to bang on the ends of the froe to force the shingle to split off. Driving wedges into the split or using a prybar would finally, after much effort, drive the froe far enough down to crack off the shake.

Broken tools and the rapidly diminishing supply of rounds slowed them down. By the end of the first day, the ten giant log rounds were gone. There were 200 shakes stacked beside the Seven Sisters antique rose bush at the front of the property.

By the next day, the shake crews had united. They took our new froes, now crumpled and warped, back to their Eastham unit. They had really taken a beating, literally. The handle on the froe had broken off. The steel shank had split and the blade had lost its sharp edge. At the unit, their talented blacksmith welded the pieces back together but it was a losing battle. The froes were eventually abandoned in favor of simple wedges and heavier sledgehammers. From then on, the shake crew consisted of the best of both teams. They spent the next six weeks turning out 2,642 shakes. To do that, we needed many, many more log rounds.

The only thing the inmates had not known to do was square the logs. They should have removed the bark and cambium layer which tend to rot more quickly in the rain and sun. That mistake would cost Neil and Mac hours of work later, running each of the shakes through a table saw to cut off the bark edges. Despite the problems, the men turned out shakes faster than anyone could supply the logs. Neil complained to Shawn that his men needed logs.

Shawn had to take up the challenge of keeping Neil's crew supplied with logs. Shawn's requested help from the city crews had met with little response. Shawn then spent every evening and all of his weekends driving the old, dilapidated city truck through the woods looking for more logs. Every morning, there had to be ten rounds on site, ready for the men to cut.

Shawn was desperate and would take almost any help he could get. Keefer pointed him into the forests but it was often hard to find long logs that were already down and dried out. One evening after a city board meeting, Shawn coerced Ralph Pease, husband of our faithful Linda Pease, into helping him load half a dozen logs out at the Gibbs forests. Ralph still reminds Shawn of his efforts.

Shawn also begged logs from Steeley Lumber, from the Gibbs Brothers, and even got some from Keefer's backyard. On one occasion, he had to dig ditches for the truck's rear tires, so that the tailgate of the truck would be low enough to roll the logs into the bed. If he had just asked me . . . but he is far too gentlemanly to ask an old schoolmarm to load logs.

Keefer Farris was a lifelong lumberman. He had worked for the Gibbs Brothers in their forests cutting lumber for much of his life. He brought twelve narrow wedges, shaped like axe heads, but thicker and not as wide. He showed the men how to place two or three of the wedges along the top of the round, hammer them in as far as they would go, then place a steel bar across the tops of the wedges and hammer that down. Once the wedges were far enough into the wood, they could pry off the shake.

It was a long and arduous task but even under the worst possible conditions, the inmates preferred it to being back at the unit. They kept on hammering out the shakes. Neil kept a daily tally on a small scrap of paper in his shirt pocket, the count growing toward 2,000.

Slowly, the cabin took shape. Mac and Neil, the now-inseparable duo, had to make choices on which logs to use and which to abandon. The fireplace wall was in bad shape. They could salvage some of the logs if the ends could be covered by a stone chimney. Since the part of the wall beyond the chimney would be clearly visible, unlike the new logs under the building, they had to use authentic logs.

Bob Bruner supplied more logs from the West Sandy property. As Bob pointed out to Mac and Neil, the same craftsman had evidently been in the West Sandy neighborhood long enough to build several buildings, including the Farris cabin. Whoever he was, he had also built buildings on the Bruner property, a church, and a schoolhouse which still stands. The adze marks on Bruner's logs were identical to those on our cabin logs. The beams were also the same size. Mac and Neil agreed to insert the replacement logs into the fireplace wall. Once they had the replacements logs, the walls went up quickly, logs stacking up, locking into place, row after row.

Once the walls were completed, the roof was next. None of the original 1930 roof materials was useable. My students and I had chopped up so many of the rafters with our attempts at roofing that Mac and Neil decided to use new pine rafters supplied by Keefer and the Gibbs Brothers Lumber Company.

The inmates stripped the bark off the long, slender logs. Just as my students and I had struggled to do a few months earlier, they put up the supports and rafters with far more elegance, ease and finesse. Mac and Neil notched the side logs along the top, nailed the two thick support beams into place, and attached the ridgepole. They nailed the rafters to the ridgepole and attached the lath to hold the shingles. Professionals can make any job look easy.

The 2,642 shakes of yellow and white oak were stacked in huge piles along the front of the property. No one had ever put on a shake roof before. Mac had seen it done at a Division of Forestry class in Montana but had not attempted it himself. The debate was not over the shakes but over the use of tar paper to keep the roof from leaking.

Shawn, Mac, Neil, Stuart, Maxia, Keefer, and Dan Phillips, a gifted local carpenter, gathered to debate the pros and cons. The tar paper would be seen from the inside and would not be historically accurate. Stuart was totally opposed. Tar paper, he said, traps the water and keeps the underside of the shakes wet, causing them to rot faster.

On the other hand, Mac and Dan argued, if the building were to be used effectively, the tar paper would keep the interior dry. The two-foot-long shakes would be overlapped by more than half their length, leaving very little of the seven-inch tar paper strips exposed from below. The anti-leak faction won the day. Now, the underside of the roof does show, here and there, and the offending tar paper does peek out.

It was at this point that Stuart noticed the problem with the shakes. The bark and growth layer, left on the edges of the shakes, would rot quickly. Neil and Mac brought in a small table saw from the museum and for the next many days, Neil stood trimming off the offending edges. The inmates began the roof along the bottom edge of the back of the roof. They nailed on a row, then tacked on the tar paper, then nailed on the next row with a deep, twelve-inch overlap. When they reached the top of both sides, the used an authentic lapping, extending the last row of shakes far up over the edge of the row on the other side of the roof. It was a technique used by early settlers who had no metal ridge rows. As Mac and Neil promised, the cabin does not leak, regardless of the intensity of the rainstorms.

Shawn had mentioned a problem with the rafters. In order to meet city codes, the rafters over the porch were too low. If the porch remained at the planned level, people entering the cabin would hit their heads on the roof. Mac and Neil, by this time, were thoroughly accustomed to the almost incessant string of requirements from the city.

Ingeniously, Mac and Neil placed a pole under the ends of the rafters. They bent the still flexible pine rafters upward the six inches necessary to provide the clearance. Keefer proudly provided old, gnarled, but still strong *bois d'arc* posts, each with a fork, to hold up the support poles. When Keefer showed us his posts, how I wished Alex and Brian had been there to see the true benefits of sturdy *bois d'arc* posts.

Like my students, all of the Eastham crew had developed an attachment to the little cabin. No longer the decrepit pile of rotting logs, the cabin again stood solid, dry and sturdy. The inmates had also received quite an education on many things beyond early Texas history, although probably not in the traditional sense.

One of the inmates was a giant of a man, easily able to lift the heaviest logs. When Neil handed him a triangular carpenter's square, however, the inmate had no idea how to use it. Briefly, the inmate struggled with the strange metal angle. Then Neil reached over and pushed the square into place and marked the straight edge across the beam. A wonderful smile of understanding -and education—lit up the inmate's face!

After having worked on the cabin for nearly six months, Christmas was fast approaching. Neil's crew completed the floors inside and the porches outside. There was still no chimney, no water, or wiring, no landscaping and no interior trim. One of the doors from the old cabin could be used, but the other two doors would have to be built by either Stuart or Keefer. Mac and Neil attached the old door to the front.

Shawn and I, as always, were left with the cleanup. We covered the other three openings with heavy plastic for the winter break. It gave me considerable pleasure to drive through town and see the little cabin dried-in, protected and solid on its foundations.

With the spring, Shawn and I organized for the final push to completion. Neil and the Eastham crew agreed to come back, and I would have another Texas History class. Shawn had already begun his "alms-for-the-poor" rounds of the city and various businesses in town. He pressured James Patton to use his influence to acquire a huge air conditioner for the cabin.

James, with his glad-handing Southern charm, convinced Beckham and Jones Heating and Air Conditioning to donate a three-ton unit for half-price, along with the installation. A log cabin with air-conditioning? It seemed ludicrous, but if Shawn's plans for the cabin were to be implemented, the small building would need air-conditioning.

Shawn had begun negotiations with several groups to use the cabin. In keeping with the primitive theme, he wanted to include only groups which produced handmade items for sale. A member from each of the groups would be responsible for keeping the cabin open to the public one or two days a week in order to sell the handmade goods produced by the members.

Shawn invited the Huntsville Spinners and Weavers Guild, and the Tall Pines Quilt Guild. Also, the Senior Center of Walker County, known as the Grandpersons' Center often had goods to sell. The Huntsville Garden Club could also use the cabin. This was the first time any of these groups would have their own sales outlet. At first hesitant, they slowly warmed to the idea as the cabin neared completion.

The landscaping was an important part of the plan. David Zellar, the city Landscape Architect, drew up a design for the surrounding land. He designated the location for the larger shrubs and trees but left the rest of the garden to Nancy Wilkens of the Waler County Garden Club. Shawn talked the city into providing truckloads of sand, clay, fill dirt and crushed granite.

James Patton had suggested the crushed granite for the walkways since it would hold up well to traffic. Shawn learned that crushed granite was available only in distant Johnson City, on the far side of Austin, and only by the eighteen-wheeler load. Shawn convinced the city to order a truckload and keep the giant mountain of granite at the Service Center. Shawn then had the city trucks bring in smaller dump truckloads to the site.

Without meaning to, the parking area for the two neighbors had dwindled considerably. Hemmed in by piles of rock, dirt, and sand, there was little room for cars. In addition, a rusty, noisy, big yellow cement mixer took up pride of place at the back of the lot.

We also needed rock for the fireplace and the gardens. Keefer told us that the Gibbs Brothers had piles of natural stone out near the Blue Lagoon, a nearby tourist site. Mac, now back at work at the museum, took time off—again—to take the city crews and their dump trucks out to the borrow pit and load up the rock. It took three trips to bring in enough rock for the lower part of the fireplace and to edge the garden.

Shawn's begging had succeeded beyond anyone's expectation. McCaffety Electric agreed to run the electric lines for lighting inside the cabin. The city crews, learning that Shawn could not be ignored, put in the water line and the water meter. Since the cabin would be a Visitor's Bureau and tourist attraction, he hoped that the Chamber of Commerce would be willing to pay for the water and electric costs. They didn't but the city did.

Shawn's greatest success was the red bricks for the walkways. He wanted authentic, antique bricks. George Russell, a local entrepreneur and collector of primitive furniture and early Texana, was the only one who owned antique bricks. George had collected the bricks from demolished old Huntsville homes. In the stacks of bricks, there were rare bricks stamped "TEXAS" and others with stars pressed into them. Many people agreed that the bricks had been made by inmates at Huntsville's prisons during the nineteenth century. The bricks were truly beyond price but Shawn insisted to George Russell that the cabin needed them.

Given the historic nature of the cabin, George finally agreed to let Shawn have the bricks. In exchange, however, he expected someone from the project to donate $400 to his Universal Ethician Church. An anonymous donor, who turned out to be Mac, donated the money and wrote the check for the full amount. Shawn had his bricks.

Neil and the Eastham crew had been delayed in returning to work on the cabin. They had been assigned to lay out a softball field, build dorms for the prison, and clean up after a tornado which had struck Trinity. Shawn was getting frantic.

That semester, I brought out my Texas History students as well as the U.S. History classes. There was little to do on the cabin but there was plenty of landscaping to do. I scheduled only two-day classes for the garden work. The Texas History students were assigned to the fireplace and the chinking. The U.S. History classes were given a purely voluntary chance to gain extra-credit.

Raking dirt, digging out rock, and breaking up concrete just didn't have quite the same excitement as moving the cabin. For the freshmen, however, it was a chance to make extra points and have fun outside of the class. As always, the students who needed the extra points were not the ones who came. Those who showed up were the A-students, so the working crew were really the best of the class. Among them was our wonderful 84-year-old Laura Johnson!

We all pitched in, laughing and joking, both the young men and women taking turns swinging the pickaxes. Laura helped too. Together, everyone dug out the rock and ran the wheelbarrows to the back of the parking lot.

We also cranked up the old yellow cement mixer to make the mud chinking to pack between the logs. We loaded in Carrol Tharpe's formula for the mud—two parts sand, two parts Portland cement, eight parts of clay and several handfuls of either hay or Spanish moss. We learned that it is difficult to judge the right amount of water. Too much water made a gooey mess that fell out from between the logs. Too little and the mud wouldn't stick.

We also learned that rubber gloves were useless. The only way to shove the mud between the chinks in the logs was bare-handed. That, of course, meant that the Portland cement dried out our hands until they cracked and peeled. The rough edges of the logs stripped our knuckles and splinters lacerated our fingers.

The Texas History class was going to learn to build a mud-cat chimney. This type of chimney is made by taking a piece of Spanish moss, approximately four inches by ten inches and packing it with mud. Lath are thin strips of wood, one inch wide by 24 inches long. The lath is nailed close together all the way up the supports of the chimney on all four sides.

The gray, muddy Spanish moss is draped all along the lath. The mud-cat, by covering the lath, protects the thin lath from the heat of the fire. As the chimney ages, however, the mud dries and flakes off the Spanish moss, exposing the lath to the flames. The old, dry moss ignites from a stray spark and the entire chimney goes up in flames. This is why most old log cabins have a gap between the chimney and the house. If the chimney burns, the homeowner can pry the burning chimney away from the house and save the logs from burning.

There were several problems with my mudcats. Like the shakes, it would have taken us about a year to do the chimney. We only had two days. The second problem was the giant metal fireplace insert which had been put in several weeks earlier.

Mac and Shawn had decided to make the fireplace usable without burning down the cabin. The metal monstrosity would have to be hidden by Shawn's rocks and not by the little mud patches. A wooden support structure would have to be built around the fire-surround to support the beams for the four sides of the chimney. Mac brought Carey Jordan, one of the museum staff members, and the two men built the wooden frame.

If we couldn't do the mud-cats, then I felt we could at least stack up a bunch of rocks to make the chimney itself. How hard could that be? The next day, we cranked up the old mixer again, and loaded the heavy sacks of cement.

Stacking rocks, even laid flat, is not easy. We tried picking the largest, smoothest rocks for the bottom layer. We oozed a little cement on the flattest part and tried to balance the next rock on top. When that didn't work, we oozed a lot of cement on top and propped the rocks on top. The cement oozed out from between the rocks. We stacked and shoved and crammed rocks and spread and dribbled and shoved in cement. By late afternoon our rickety rock wall was about a foot and a half high, still some four feet from the top of the fire-surround. We wiped off the tools, washed out the wheelbarrow, but no one remembered to wash out the mixer.

The next day, to our immense thankfulness, Neil and his crew returned at last. Neil had requested a man from one of the other work crews at Eastham. He was a real stone mason. He tried to look polite when he saw our rock wall. He and the inmates pulled down our rocks and hammered out the dried chunks of cement from the inside of the mixer. The inmates had to hammer on the outside of the mixer and bang away inside with a long, heavy prybar to break lose the chunks of cement that had adhered to the inner walls and the mixer blade.

Within a week, the stone mason had reconstructed the rock wall around the fireplace. He carefully fitted the rocks together, all standing on edge instead of sitting on each other. He meticulously placed the cement between them to hold the rocks in place. He had to wait to let the cement dry after each day's work, but the rock wall went up quickly and efficiently. While he finished the chimney, the rest of the crew finished the landscaping. They finished digging out the rocks and old concrete, dredged a pond, and spread the granite.

As part of the landscaping, Shawn had the inmates install the antique bricks in front of the cabin. Neil and Mac marked out a semicircle and the two arms of the walkway, based on the design by David Zellar. The surface would not be completely smooth, since the bricks would have to follow the contours of the drainage swales, put in to prevent flooding. With considerable skill and artistry, the inmates laid out the bricks, with the stars and TEXAS bricks prominently displayed. They cemented then into place. The effect of the red brick entry was warm and welcoming—and appropriately historic.

The men from Beckham and Jones arrived to install the air-conditioner. It was conveniently hidden behind the rock fireplace. Using an almost matching brown paint, Shawn spray-painted the air-handling unit and the return air duct s leading into and out of the building. The brown blended with the walls of the cabin, as much as could be expected. Inside we covered the pipes with chinking mud and painted the grills with brown paint.

To keep the cool air from leaking out, we chinked the cracks in the gable ends of the roof. There was nothing we could do about the holes in the roof between the shakes. The larger open knotholes in the gable ends also had to be covered. Shawn had been promised some old, rusty tin-can tops to cover the knotholes. When they didn't materialize, we used the old tin license plates from the original roof, still clearly reading 1933.

Mac and Neil also debated the advisability of skirting the building. George Russell and Stuart were opposed, since it was not historic. Where would the chickens and pigs have lived if they couldn't get under the house? That was exactly the point, countered Mac and Neil. They did not want pigs, chickens, snakes, racoons or any other kind of varmints making their homes under the cabin. The argument for air circulation, however, made more sense. Mac and Neil designed the skirting with mesh air holes. The inmates finished the skirting. Mac built the requisite ADA wheelchair ramp at the museum and brought it back to the cabin. The inmates installed it at the back of the cabin.

I was still half-heartedly insisting that my students do the mud-cats on the upper part of the chimney. Mac and Neil wisely ignored my requests and finished the chimney with mud to match the rest of the chinking between the logs. One of the inmates, a plasterer in a past life, called for fiberboard backing and screen mesh. They tacked it onto the wooden chimney supports and up through the roof. Within a day, the plasterer had covered the chimney with a rough coat of mud. So much for the mud-cats, but the chimney did look good.

Someone had provided a small mantel for the fireplace. Keefer objected. He brought a long piece of beautiful, thick, black walnut. It was unfinished and not cut to size but the wood was magnificent. Mac took the wood home. He used up several saw blades cutting the mantel into shape. He planed and sanded it, then polished it, hand-rubbing oil into the rich dark wood. He completed the piece by adding matching brackets from the leftover wood. Then he quietly but proudly installed the magnificent mantel over the fireplace.

As we neared completion, Shawn learned that McCaffety Electric needed bigger conduits to run their lines. Of course, the conduit lay under one corner of the brick walk. At least it was not under the cabin. Cursing mildly, Neil had the inmates rip up the brick and re-lay the conduit.

With the last chore accomplished, Neil and his crew returned to the Eastham Unit in Lovelady. They had done what none of us could have done. But they, too, had learned to care for the little cabin. Upon their release at the nearby Walls Unit, many of them have returned with their families. Like the students who have also returned, they have all pointed with justified pride at the lovely little cabin on the square that would not have existed without them.

Shawn had chosen May 4th for the final dedication of the cabin. It was held on the First Annual Airing of the Quilts, an appropriately historic event. Hundreds of brightly colored quilts hung all over the town square. The Quilters Guild displayed their best quilts hanging from the rafters of the cabin. The Spinners and Weavers, wheels spinning and looms clacking rhythmically on the front porch, laid out the woven scarves and shawls for sale. The Senior Center displayed their bags and crafts.

The Firefighters were also holding a fund raiser in the street out front. The large crowd on hand witnessed the passing of the keys to the new caretakers. There were still many things to do in those last few days, but the cabin was put to use.

Shawn's family arrived for the opening and Shawn pressed his father into service. Together they brought in the primitive furniture from George Russell's collection. It did wrench his father's back in the process, but we didn't have Lynette to help. The rest of the final touches waited until the following week.

Those last few days, we clambered up and down ladders, mounting the hidden track lighting. We installed locks on the doors and finished the last of the chinking. We swept and cleaned the floor and rearranged the furniture. The new incumbents could move it to suit themselves.

On the last night, as the wisps of evening clouds turned from white to gold to pink in the deepening twilight, Shawn and I sat on the front porch leaning against Keefer's gnarled *bois d'arc* posts. We laughed over all the crazy stories. So many had said we couldn't do it. Shawn got up periodically, like a nervous father to smooth out the granite and sweep up a few leaves that strayed onto the brick. We might have handed over the cabin to new users, but it would always belong to all of those who had worked on it.

The Cabin on the Square had touched all of our lives in a way none of us could have imagined. The logs were permeated with memories. Its history had infected us. The past had slowly seeped into us as we worked around the cabin. As dusk settled, we sat quietly, absorbing the immensity of the cabin's past. We had passed it on to the future, to other visitors.

ADDENDUM

The Cabin remained on the town square for ten years. In the end, the Smither family determined to use the property for a food truck. Shawn Lewis was gone but I was still around. I was upset at the request since, regrettably, our little cabin would no longer sit with pride on the town square. It would no longer provide a home for the sale of historic, hand-made goods in Huntsville.

At the time, fortunately, Mac Woodward had been elected Mayor of Huntsville. The Smithers gave him six weeks to remove the cabin. Calling on the city's workforce, he again used large tow-trucks to move the cabin from the square. This time, of course, the cabin was solid and was moved without much drama. The chimney was lost, as was the electrical and air conditioning, but the logs stayed intact.

Using his contacts with Museum Director Pat Nolan, Mac asked to move the cabin onto the museum grounds. Pat agreed. Today, the Roberts-Farris cabin has joined a number of other historic buildings on the museum grounds. It looks less imposing on the museum grounds, but it is still our little cabin and all of those who worked on it can still visit it for old time's sake.

PART II
The Background

CHAPTER 5

The Farris Family from 1756 to 2001

By Laura Johnston with Maggie Farris Parker

It was a very warm day in the middle of July 2001 when I first saw the log cabin in a cow pasture located off FM 1791 near Huntsville, Texas. It looked so lonesome sitting there in the midst of the breeze-swept grasses, partially shaded at one corner by an Osage orange tree and a rampant trumpet vine clambering up a porch support. My feeling of isolation and remoteness was interrupted by the distant lowing of a cow. Then I noticed the chirping of crickets, hundreds of them, followed by the call of a bird. There was life all around me, but not the kind to which I was accustomed.

The cabin was a one-pen, eighteen-square-foot house of notched logs built 160 years ago. Through the years, however, add-on sheds and a front porch had more than doubled the living space. I wondered about all the people who had lived there over all those decades.

Hezekiah Farris was born in Virginia in 1797, and first came to Texas in 1835. He had learned of the opportunity to stake a claim for free land. Hezekiah found an area to his liking in what would later be called Walker County, at the headwaters of the west fork of the San Jacinto River. He returned to Tennessee to gather his family.

Before they could move to Texas, the strong and persistent rumors of a war between the Texas colonists and Mexico changed his plans. He and a number of his friends from Franklin County, including Captain

James Gillespie, gathered up their long-rifles and a few belongings, and rushed back to Texas to join the fray.

Before their arrival back in Texas, the war for Texas Independence had broken out. On March 2, 1836, Texas had declared its independence from Mexico. Mexico's leader, Antonio Lopez de Santa Anna, with over three thousand men at his command, was determined to stop the colonist's revolt. He marched resolutely from Mexico City toward the Alamo mission in San Antonio. The battle for the Alamo lasted almost two weeks, and on March 6, 1836, Santa Anna overwhelmed the 187 Texians defending the fort. All of the Texian soldiers died fighting, including Colonel William Barret Travis, commander of the garrison; David Crockett; James Bowie; and James B. Bonham.

While Santa Anna captured San Antonio, his second-in-command, General Urrea attacked the settlement at Goliad where he captured General Fannin and his men. At Santa Anna's orders, General Urrea executed the prisoners who had surrendered to him following the battle of Coleto Creek. When word of this defeat and brutal slaughter of those 330 Texians spread across the land, the colonists' already inflamed passions became polarized. The men and boys joined the Texas army under the command of General Sam Houston.

Sam Houston's appointment as general had met little resistance from the Republic's newly formed congress. He had come to Texas from Tennessee just four years earlier, but with his commanding physical presence, his training as a lawyer, and his experience of having been a U.S. senator from Tennessee, he was quickly chosen to head up this new rebelling colony's army.

By mid-April of 1836, he had recruited 900 men including forty from Tennessee, along with Hezekiah Faris and Captain James Gillespie. Hezekiah Faris served in the 2nd Regiment, 5th Company under Captain James Gillespie from March 1, 1836, to May 30, 1836 with service number 6561.

Stalling for time in order to gain numerical strength, Houston led his men on forced marches long the coastal plains, desperate to stay ahead of Santa Anna. The Mexican army caught up with General Houston and his troops at a spot called San Jacinto, a short distance east of Harrisburg (today Houston). Santa Anna set up camp there to rest and prepare for the next days' battle. General Houston was very much aware of where his enemy was encamped, and of their numbers. He recognized that surprise might be his best ally. Accordingly, at 2:00 on the afternoon of April 21, 1836, Houston's men attacked Santa Anna's camp with great shouts of "Remember the Alamo!" and "Remember Goliad!" Firing rifles, side-arms and their two six-pounder cannons, the Texian soldiers caused panic in the Mexican encampment. Within a few minutes, the Texians had the napping Mexican soldiers running for their lives. By three o'clock, the Mexicans were soundly defeated and massacred.

According to J. W. Winters, a veteran of the battle, "Houston gave orders to form in line and march back to camp, but [we] paid no attention to him, as [we were] all shaking hands and rejoicing over the victory. Houston gave the order three times and still the men paid no attention to him. And he turned his horse around and said, 'Men, I can gain victories with you, but damn your manners,' and rode on to camp."

Over 700 prisoners were taken, but their leader, Santa Anna, was not one of them. The Texians scattered to round up prisoners. Family tradition has it that late in the afternoon, Hezekiah and two other soldiers spotted a man crawling through the bushes. They dismounted from their horses, selected Hezekiah to stand under the brush cover and hold the horses while the other two crawled up to capture the prisoner. Somewhat later, they returned to camp with their captives. Upon reaching camp, the other prisoners began to stand and salute their leader with cries of "El General!" "El General!" It was then the Texians realized just who one of those captives really was: Santa Anna! With the success of this battle, the Republic of Texas was born.

As a reward for participating in this battle, Hezekiah was given a grant for a section of land, 640 acres, and he returned to the area he had picked out a few months earlier. He then returned once more to Tennessee to pack up his family and their belongings for the move to the new Republic of Texas and a fresh start. His two single brothers, William and Richard, joined him as traveling companions on the journey to Texas. Others from Franklin County interested in settling in Texas joined them. The group arrived by boat in Galveston.

In 1837 the group traveled overland by oxcart more than sixty miles to their new home sites. He filed his claim on July 15, 1838, for grant number 464 on the South side of the West Fork of the San Jacinto River, in what today is Walker County.

Hezekiah's family consisted of his wife, Matilda Stevens Roberts Faris, whom he had married several years earlier. Their two children were James Morgan, born October 28, 1832, and Susan, born October 18, 1835. Joining the group later was Matilda's grown son from a previous marriage, Allen Roberts and his wife, Henrietta Guerrant, and their two children. Five more children were later born in Texas. With the group was Henrietta's seventeen-year-old brother Daniel Boone Anderson Guerrant, many of whose descendants still live in Walker County. Allen Robertson, stepson to Hezekiah Faris, was the builder and original owner of the cabin whose history we are studying.

The new settlers came with zeal and enthusiasm and a willingness to work hard to change this vast empire of virgin forests into plowed land and pastures. They named their new community "Goshen" after their hometown in Tennessee. "There is much truth in the claim that the men and women who had lived through the perils of this time and successfully staked out homes in the wilderness were of heroic mold. Cowards never started and weaklings died by the wayside. We salute these pioneers."

The Hezekiah Faris lineage has been traced back to the mid-1700s in Goochland County, Virginia. It was there that his grandfather, Richard Faris moved the family, consisting of seven boys and one girl, to Louisa County, Virginia. After the death of Elizabeth, Richard married Susannah Shelton, and he later died in Virginia.

Richard Faris, the sixth son of Richard and Elizabeth, was born in 1765. At the age of forty-three, he and several of his brothers migrated to Franklin County, Tennessee. All of them purchased land and settled down with their families. On September 6, 1827, Richard Faris offered a 150+ acre tract of land on the Elk River to his two sons, Hezekiah and James. In return the boys agreed to cancel a debt of $200 owed them by their father. As part of the agreement, the sons promised to support their father and mother for the rest of their natural lives. Nine years later, evidently after the death of their father, Hezekiah left Tennessee and brought his family to Texas.

The Goshen community grew rapidly as other settlers migrated to the area and built their log cabin homes. Soon Hezekiah realized the need for a place of worship. With his neighbors, he selected a site on the North Bank of Sandy Creek. In 1841, the members of the Goshen community built a crude log building for the church. Several years later, it was discovered that the two acres belonged to Mr. and Mrs. John T. Myrix. The couple deeded the land to the church on August 15, 1859, and received twenty dollars for the land. At the dedication ceremony for the small chapel, Mr. Spillers moved that since Hezekiah Faris had proposed and founded the church and donated the logs, it should be named for him.

The motion passed, and Hezekiah named the little church 'Faris Chapel,' in memory of another small Methodist Church back home in Franklin County, Tennessee also named Faris Chapel. The Trustees for the chapel were N. A. Sims, Sr., William Mills, Jr., MacGruder Wynne, J. W. Mayes and L. W. Wilson Jr. Hezekiah served as chairman.

The Methodist, Presbyterian, and Baptist denominations worshipped there. For all of the congregation, the nearby flowing creek was convenient for watering their horses, and, during the summertime, for holding their baptism services. A nearby spring provided water for drinking, as well as cooking during the annual two-week summer revivals. By 1869, the chapel also served as a schoolhouse on weekdays. There were no taxes to cover the salary for a teacher (or for a building or its upkeep). The community members raised donations to cover these costs. This was the first school established in the county.

Early lists of teachers and students indicate that the chapel was well used. Some of the early teachers were Mrs. Stakes, Mr. Crow, Mr. Derick, and Minnie Hunter. More recent teachers included Miss Rosa Bowden, Miss Fanne Elkins, Mr. Edd Curtis, Mr. Edd McKay, Miss Mary Stern, and Miss Alice Farris. The school terms lasted from three to five months.

Among the students were Howell Mayes, John Roberts, Dock Sims, N. O. Sims, Sally Sims, John David Walker, Jim Walker, Bill Walker, Charlotte Welch, Sarah Welch, Ruth Burnett, Julian Burnett, Annie Farris, Nannie Cox, Mary Ann Cox, Mary Hill, Nora Mayes, Susan Gillespie and James Hezekiah Farris.

Hezekiah's two children, Susan and James, both settled in the small community. Susan married Captain James Gillespie, her father's old friend from Tennessee. Although Gillespie was thirty years her senior, the couple had a large family of which five survived.

Hezekiah's son, James Morgan, married Susan Elizabeth Browne on February 26, 1860. She is given credit for the addition of a second "r" to the Faris name. Susan Elizabeth was born in Monroe County, Alabama, on October 18, 1833. She had migrated to Texas with her family sometime during the years of the Republic. James and Susan had six children: Matilda Ann, James Hezekiah, William Edward, Robert Lee, Allen Browne, and Mary Alice Susan.

Just after his marriage to Susan, James Morgan Farris joined the Confederacy during the Civil War. In 1862-63, during his second winter away from home, Susan and their first daughter, Matilda Ann, struggled to survive on parched corn kernels. After James' return to Texas, he served as a private in the Texas State Police.

After the war, James carried out Hezekiah's wishes to rebuild the small chapel. Over the years, the community had outgrown the log cabin church. It had begun to deteriorate and weather. James helped build a new church around 1880, a building which has lasted over one hundred years. During the 1980s, a new brick building was constructed, with air-conditioning and a centrally heated sanctuary, but the old building remained. With the exception of a few years during the Civil war, the community members have held weekly church services continuously since 1841.

James Morgan Farris died of "congestion of the brain" in the spring of 1887 at the age of fifty-five. Just ten months later, on January 3, 1888, his wife, Susan, died of yellow fever. Susan's death made orphans of their five sons and daughters. Matilda Ann, the eldest, had already married. The two older boys, James Hezekiah and William Edward, were twenty-four and twenty-two at the time. The brothers took on the responsibility to make a living for their three younger siblings. They took jobs in the copper mines in Arizona which paid on a monthly basis. William Edward was killed in a mine accident on May 2, 1892. Shortly thereafter, James Hezekiah returned to the Goshen community where he settled down as a farmer and rancher to care for his siblings. Fortunately for all concerned, Bob, Brown and Mary Alice, then eighteen, fifteen and thirteen years-old respectively, received scholarships to attend Westminster College, a Methodist Protestant School at Tehuacana, a small town in East Texas.

James "Jim" Hezekiah Farris married Maggie Guerrant, daughter of Daniel Boone Anderson Guerrant, on June 21, 1896. The couple had five children: Jimmy, Lee Elwin, Edward Quincy, Alton Boone, and Marion Hezekiah, better known by his nickname "Kye." Again, in this generation, an untimely death of a parent caused upheaval in the family. Maggie Guerrant Farris was only forty-four and had given birth just ten days before to the youngest child, Kye, when she died on March 28, 1916. Her other four children ranged in age from nineteen to twelve years old. James Hezekiah arranged with Matilda Ann Faris Bruner, his older sister, to take the baby to raise. Matilda, married to James Bruner, lived on the land adjoining the Farris property. Jimmy, the eldest, was sent to town to attend college at Sam Houston Normal Institute. James and his three sons, Lee, Quincy, and Alton continued to live at the home place and to work the farm. In 1918, James Hezekiah courted and won the hand of Maggie Fowler, a charming lady hat stylist working in a dry goods store in Huntsville. She moved to the farm and Baby Kye, now aged two, rejoined the family. James and Maggie continued to live on the land but had no children of their own.

Lee Elwin Farris married Eva Mae Roberts, a descendant of Allen Roberts. They built their home on a portion of the Hezekiah Faris land grant. They had two children, and a third child died and is buried at Farris Cemetery. After their home burned in 1930, the couple moved to Huntsville, where two additional children were born during the Depression.

Alton was the only one of the siblings to remain on the family farm. Starting in the early 1930s, the cabin was moved on several occasions. It served to accommodate sharecroppers and later tenant farmers. First, however, the fireplace was rebuilt using a clay, hay, and water compound. The same material was used to chink the cracks between the logs. A shed-like kitchen area was erected adjacent to the back door. A front porch was added and then the money ran out. This was in the midst of the Great Depression and even small dollar expenditures weighed heavily on the family budget. Alton learned that unsold 1933 car license plates were available from the prison system for free. He quickly availed himself of a truckload of them which he turned into shingles to make a roof covering for the new porch.

Several years earlier, on a Sunday afternoon in the summer of 1927, Alton was cruising the streets of Huntsville in his snappy new Model T. He caught the eye of Erma Keefer, one of the Sam Houston co-eds. Erma, the youngest child of Maxia and Mary Keefer from North Zulch, Texas, was under strict orders to have no traffic with unknown young men, especially those who might have intentions of luring her away from her studies. Alton and Erma's clandestine meetings did not reach the ears of the Keefer family. In the Fall of 1927, Erma was offered a teaching job in a small school at Normangee, Texas. She accepted but Alton continued to call almost every weekend. On November

11, 1927, Erma and Alton eloped. She quit her job at Normangee and the young couple moved in with James Hezekiah and Maggie, better known as "Auntie," until they could build their own home just down the hill.

Although Erma obviously had many appealing attributes, her cooking ability was not one of them. Once ensconced in her own home and kitchen, she set about preparing her first supper for her husband. Alton was away working a day-job at the time. The only thing Erma knew how to make was a lemon pie, and so she did. Nothing else. That night, Alton dutifully ate his ¾ share, leaving the rest for her. There were no doubt, some serious adjustments made before the next supper time.

Over the next nine years, and through the midst of the Great Depression, four children were born: Maggie, Truell, Keefer, and Maxia. Alton, with the help of a succession of tenant farmers, and his wife and the older children, continued to work the farm and their cattle. During these years he also held several seasonal jobs working out of the AAA office in town, first as a land surveyor in the federal cotton subsidy program and later rounding up cattle to be disinfected and protected against ticks. During this period, the primary cash crop for farmers in the South was cotton and the price was dropping lower every year. At last, the Federal Government came up with a plan to encourage farmers not to plant as many acres as the year before.

Alton was hired to travel around the county measuring crops and fields to determine the amount of government subsidy was due to each of the farmers. Later, in conjunction with a federal program intended to diminish state-wide infestations of cattle tick, he rode a horse for miles each day to help round up herds and move them through the dipping vats.

Throughout this time, the family subsisted primarily on whatever they grew on their own farm or what they could find in the wild. Fruits, vegetables, chickens and hogs came from their farm. Erma learned to sew skirts, shirts and blouses from cotton sacking material.

Maggie once noted, in reference to their family's economic status during the era, "We were poor, but I didn't know it until someone pointed it out to me in high school."

During the nine-month school year, the three older children, Maggie, Truett, and Keefer, walked the one and a half miles to school in the heat, cold or rain. By contrast, when the family was dressed in their Sunday best and ready for church, which was a quarter of a mile down the road, they always drove the car.

By the time Maxia, the baby of the family, was ready to go to school, a providential inheritance allowed the family to build in Huntsville and move to town. Erma and Maggie enrolled at Sam Houston College together. Maggie, attending year-round, finished with majors in business and education and graduated in July 1948. She moved to Houston and worked at Foley's Department store for the next five years. She married A. T. "Buzz" Ryden and had two children, Sandra and Alan. From 1970 to 1993, she worked as Director of Children's Ministries at the Memorial Drive United Methodist Church. Two years after retiring, and some six years after the death of her first husband, Maggie married George E. Parker.

Erma, the children's mother, graduated in 1949, earning her BA in Education. She continued her studies and in 1952, received her Masters in Library Science. After receiving this degree, Erma returned to teaching and working as a librarian in schools at Cleveland, Conroe, and Brenham, Texas.

In the years from 1949 through 1968, while Alton continued to raise cattle on the farm, the three sons enrolled at Sam Houston College and all of then eventually earned degrees. Truett married Sara Terrell from Georgia. He served a two-year stint in the U.S. Army, including a year in Korea. He returned from the war and earned his Graphic Arts degree in 1954. Two years later, in 1965, the couple adopted their only child, Terrell Eleanor Farris. Truett's career has been spent in the newspaper publishing business in Bay City, Texas.

In 1948, Keefer completed a degree in Physical Education. He married Naomi Voyles of Idabel, Oklahoma. The couple returned to Huntsville where they reared their two children, Alton and Ruth. His occupations have ranged from running a pulpwood operation to employment with the Texas Prison System as Director of Physical Education for one of the units.

Maxia married Rochelle McCollum, a Huntsville native. The couple had two boys, Terry and Troy. Both Maxia and Rochelle attended Sam Houston, Maxia finishing a degree in Education in 1958, and later, a Masters in Education. Rochelle obtained her degree in Education. Both taught in the public schools for several years until Maxia accepted a position with the Texas Department of Criminal Justice Educational System. His job was to direct education programs which offered inmates training and experience in car maintenance, upholstery, furniture-making and refinishing, TV repair, and more.

In 1973, Erma retired, and she and Alton built a new home on their farm in West Sandy. They sold their home in Huntsville and moved back to the farm. Not long afterward, they hired a surveyor to measure and divide the 300-acre farm into four equal portions. On a Sunday afternoon they invited the children to gather at the farm. Each of the four drew straws to determine which section of the land they would receive. Deeds were drawn up and the titles transferred. The children understood that Alton and Erma would continue to raise cattle and live out their lives on the family farm in the home they had built.

Maggie drew the straw representing Section two, the acreage where the cabin sat. In 1984, while lunching with her mother at the Homestead Restaurant in Huntsville, she saw the potential for this long unused cabin. It had to be moved to a location where people had access to it. Accordingly, she began a campaign to get the Walker County Historical Commission to take the cabin and move it into town. Meanwhile, she had asked her brothers if they would join in this family venture whereby the gift of the cabin would be made in all their names. The family agreed and the Farris descendants donated the cabin to the City of Huntsville and the citizens of Walker County in August 2001, in hopes that future generations would learn a little of the life and times of early citizens of Walker County, Texas.

ALLEN ROBERTS FAMILY

by Lucille Farris Benthall

Note: The following information comes from the *Huntsville and Walker County, Texas: A Bicentennial History,* edited by D'Anne McAdams Crews (Huntsville, TX: Sam Houston State University 1976), p. 263. The material was submitted by Ms. Benthall, although she was not a student in the Texas History class. Her information completed the information on the Roberts-Farris cabin.

—

Thomas Roberts married Matilda Stevens in Georgia. They had four children. Matilda Stevens was born January 21, 1788; she died December 15, 1865, and is buried in the Farris Cemetery in Walker County, Texas. Thomas Roberts died in Tennessee, leaving Matilda a widow.

Allen Roberts was born in Georgia to Thomas Roberts and Matilda Stevens Roberts on May 17, 1810; and died in Walker County, Texas on November 5, 1879 ; he is buried in Farris Cemetery. He married Henrietta Judith Guerrant in Franklin County, Tennessee on October 22, 1834. She was the daughter of Charles and Martha Spencer Guerrant. Henrietta was born September 15, 1814, and died November 7, 1855. She is also buried in Farris Cemetery, Walker County, Texas.

After their marriage, Allen and Henrietta Judith, along with her brother Daniel Boone Guerrant, age seventeen, and the two Roberts children, born in Tennessee, Edwin James and Elizabeth, then decided to go to the much talked about Spanish Territory in Texas. Allen Roberts was seeking his mother, the former Mrs. Thomas Roberts who had become a widow and married Hezekiah Farris in Tennessee. (For further information concerning Matilda Stevens Roberts see Hezekiah Farris and descendants. Also, for further information see Daniel B. Guerrant).

Allen and Henrietta with their children and Daniel B. Guerrant, her brother, came by boat to Galveston and settled in Montgomery County near his mother Matilda Stevens Robert Farris, approximately fifteen miles from Huntsville in the year of 1837. Anson Jones, President of the Republic of Texas, granted Allen and his wife 640 acres of land in June 1842. Also, her brother Daniel Guerrant received 320 acres being a single man. A few years later Daniel Guerrant married and his daughter Margaret "Maggie" married James Hezekiah Farris (a grandson of Hezekiah Farris). These land grants were near the Hezekiah Farris survey. On this tract of land Allen and Henrietta Roberts cleared away the forest and then built a three-room log house. The house had been moved from its original location and is presently located on its third site, not far from the original building site. Allen Roberts planted crepe myrtle and walnut trees that still bloom and bear fruit at his old homesite. Allen Roberts sold his homesite to James Morgan Farris, November 23, 1858; at a later date his heirs sold the remaining land to James Morgan Farris on January 30, 1884. (Note: Miss Mayme B. Farris, of Dallas, was born July 16, 1898, in the old Allen Roberts log house; her parents were Robert Lee and Fleta Bradley Farris.) Allen and Henrietta Judith had eight children. Seven were listed on the 1850 census report: Edwin James, Elizabeth, George Guinn, William, Thomas, Ann and John.

CHAPTER 6

The Land and Property of the Roberts-Farris Cabin

By Thomas Vanderberg

The Piney Woods of East Texas impart a sense of beauty and serenity. The undulation of the hills combined with the grandeur of the mighty pine forests rising from the fertile soil leaves an impression of majesty and awe. These superficial images account for all of the knowledge some visitors have of the area, despite its rich historical legacy. Except for the occasional historical marker or historical site noted on a map, many people pass through the area without knowing the history of the area or the hard work of generations of residents to tame the land. The Farris family and their log cabin serve as but one example of the intriguing past of Walker County. In order to truly understand the history of the cabin, one must trace the history of the property.

Many of the important historical sites which relate to the Roberts-Farris Cabin still remain intact. Each of these structures built on or around the property forms an integral part of the history of the Farris property.

The sojourn begins along present-day Farm-to-Market Road (F.M.) 1791, approximately twelve miles south of Highway 30, west of Huntsville, Texas. On the corner of the intersection between F.M.

1791 and F.M. 3179 stands a broken-down white building boasting two good-sized rooms and a large hall with a modest stage. This structure served as one of the first three schools in the area.

In the early 1900s, the San Jacinto Public School opened its doors to educate local children. San Jacinto Public School was not the only school in the area. Frog Joy school, which opened in the late 1800s or early 1900s in the northwest corner of the Gill Survey, also educated local youngsters in the rudiments of education. Alton Farris attended the Frog Joy school as a child.

During the early 1900s, the San Jacinto school consisted of twelve to fourteen classrooms in a two-storied structure, a stylish gymnasium and a playground fully equipped with swings and seesaws. As Huntsville grew and more children moved to town, the structure was dismantled shortly after World War II. It was replaced with a two-room schoolhouse connected to a small auditorium, which probably also served as the lunchroom. This is the very dilapidated structure that still stands across the road from Ebenezer Baptist Church at the intersection of F.M. 1791 and F.M. 3179 today.

Equally important to Texans in the 1880s was religious salvation. The Farris Chapel is a prime example of an institution that provided a haven for those seeking religion. After Hezekiah Farris procured his headright of 640 acres from the Republic of Texas government, he helped build a small log chapel and established a Methodist congregation in 1841. The congregation thrived even after Hezekiah's death in 1859.

In 1880, Hezekiah's son and the church congregation built a second building, the old Farris Chapel, which still stands today. Other religious denominations shared the edifice, and the building served as the first area schoolhouse—preceding Frog Joy and San Jacinto Public School.

West Sandy Creek used to run slightly closer to the church building. Over time, however, the creek's path has changed. In the early days of the chapel's existence, the congregation ventured only a few yards behind the church to carry out baptisms in the waters of the West Sandy. Although the original chapel still stands, a new church building has been erected and houses regular church services, while the old Farris Chapel has been relegated to the role of storage facility.

The Farris Cemetery lies less than a mile south of the Farris Chapel. In 1842, death came to the small community thriving along the West Sandy. Since no cemetery existed, Hezekiah donated an acre of his property to serve as the community cemetery. According to historical legend, "the first person to be buried here was a slave."

Hezekiah's son, James Morgan Farris, and his wife took charge of overseeing the cemetery after Hezekiah's death. They started the tradition of "Graveyard Working," an annual communal event the last Tuesday in July. Local families gathered to maintain the cemetery with landscaping and cleaning the grounds. After the chores were completed, "the ladies of the church spread their lunches together and all enjoyed the good food and hour of visiting with their neighbors." This tradition still remains intact today.

As the plots filled, the Farris family added to the size of the cemetery. In 1925, James Hezekiah Farris gave another acre, and George and Jimmy Kearse deeded another 1.5 acres in 1948. Today, the cemetery consists of "about 7 acres belonging to the Farris Cemetery Association." Like many historical cemeteries across East Texas, the Farris Cemetery provides a serene and gorgeous resting place for all of the descendants of the original settlers. Interested individuals may contact the Farris Cemetery Association for more information.

The Roberts-Farris Cabin, immediately before its move to the Huntsville Main Square, was located in the southwest corner of a 20.4-acre tract of land bordering the Hezekiah Farris Survey (A-207) as a part of the Frederick Elms Survey (A-175). West Sandy Creek runs through the pasture on the north side. A hill slopes down toward the north, allowing the runoff to fill the creek.

The northernmost acreage used to be marshland until Alton Farris cleared the bog with dynamite to increase drainage and gain acreage covered by the quagmire. Trees line the West Sandy as it winds through the landscape, and beavers and deer make their homes in the shady oasis. Fresh, cool natural springs once gushed across the area. As more and more residents built water wells, however, the springs have dried up and finally stopped flowing.

The Roberts-Farris cabin was not always located on the 20.4-acre tract owned by Maggie Farris Ryden Parker. Allen Roberts first constructed the cabin sometime during the 1840s, using well-hewn logs and half-dovetail notches. He built the cabin on the western edge of the Hezekiah Farris survey. A black walnut tree and several crepe myrtle trees still stand near the original Roberts cabin site. This land is now owned by Lucille Farris Benthall.

From this spot, the cabin was moved approximately 1000 feet to the east-northeast after Roberts gave the cabin to Hezekiah. Each time the cabin was moved, except for the move from the countryside to the Huntsville Main Square, it was disassembled and moved log by log.

The Farris family moved the cabin sometime during the beginning of the twentieth century. The cabin was rebuilt on a hill located in the southeast corner of a 50.6-acre tract presently owned by Sandra Ryden Wilson, daughter of Maggie Farris Parker, and borders the Hezekiah Farris Survey. This spot is easily recognized by the peach tree that grew next to the cabin during its tenure on the hilltop. On the top of the hill the family could enjoy the cool summer breezes and gaze out upon the low, rolling hills of the surrounding countryside.

The cabin was moved to its final location on the property sometime prior to 1933— evident from the dates on the license plates used to construct one of the shed roofs. The Farris's, or their tenants, added a total of three side rooms and a porch on the front. After the last tenant family moved out in 1940, the Farris family converted the cabin into a cow crib. The cabin remained a hay barn until the turn of the century in 2001.

The 20.4-acre tract owned by Maggie Farris Ryden Parker has changed hands many times over the past 160 years. On December 5,

1844, Hezekiah Faris (also Fares)—the spelling would later change to Farris—received a patent for a land grant of 640 acres in what would become Walker County. This survey carries abstract number 207 and Hezekiah Farris's name. Hezekiah bought additional land over time. In 1858, William W. Leonard sold land to Allen Roberts, Matilda Farris' child from a previous marriage. He had also migrated to Texas with the Farris family. Deed records indicate that Roberts paid the sum of $500 "in two promissory notes, one for two-hundred and fifty dollars payable on the first day of January one thousand eight-hundred and fifty-nine. The other, due the first day of January one thousand eight-hundred and sixty-two for two hundred and fifty dollars." Land records are often confusing and hard to decipher. In this case, the 204-acre tract was defined in the following terms:

> *Beginning on the Western boundary said Elms headright at a Stake from which a Post Oak 16 in. in dia. Bears S 23 E 11 12/10 varas and a black oak 8 in. in dia... E 2110 [sic] varas [a form of measurement] Thence S 49 30" West with the Southern boundary of Said headright 721 6/10 varas to the S West Corner of Said Frederick Elms Survey... With the western boundary of Said survey 722 8/10 varas to the Beginning.*

Trees grow, stakes decay and creeks change course—but legal surveys remain. The 20.4-acre lot in question was part of a deed between James Hezekiah Farris and Alton Farris which states that the property was "part of the Frederick Elms league and fully described in a deed from W. W. Leonard to Allen Roberts, which is recorded in Vol. E, page ninety-seven, of the deed records of Walker County Texas." When Alen Roberts died in 1814, he bequeathed the property to his half-brother, James Morgan Farris, who, in turn, passed it to his son, James Hezekiah.

In 1926, James Hezekiah Farris passed the land to Alton Farris, "as part of the estate of his deceased mother Maggie Farris." Alton's four children, Maggie, Truett, Keefer, and Maxia, divided the land among themselves in 1970 by drawing straws. Keefer receiver 71.05

acres "more or less," Maggie Farris Ryden received "20.44 acres being out of a one hundred acre tract in the Fred Elms survey," and Maxia received "71-05/100 acres of land, or less out of the W. C. Gill Survey." Truett received the remainder. The cabin was located on the property that Maggie Farris Ryden Parker received.

Maggie Farris Ryden Parker still owns the land, but she and her brothers have donated the cabin to the City of Huntsville and to Walker County. Today, the cabin sits on property owned by the Smither family on the Huntsville Main Square. This land originally is believed to have belonged to Pleasant Gray, the first settler of Huntsville.

CHAPTER 7

Pleasant Gray

Father of Huntsville

By Susan B. Locklear

Pleasant Gray, the founder of Huntsville, Texas, was born June 15, 1806, in Tennessee. He grew up near Huntsville, Alabama according to the Gray family Bible and family records. Jury lists for Tipton County, Tennessee in 1826, lists Pleasant and his brother Ephraim and indicate that they had been out of the area, returning to Tennessee during this period.

By his early twenties, Pleasant Gray had become an active member of the Tipton County community. The United States Census of 1830 for Tennessee lists Pleasant Gray, his wife, Hannah, and one child under the age of five residing in Tipton County, Tennessee. Hannah was born on March 4, 1809, in North Carolina and later moved to Tennessee with her family. Family records indicate that Pleasant and Hannah married June 15, 1826. Their first son, Michael, was born on April 1, 1827, and John A. W. Gray, their second son, was born June 11, 1830, after the census was taken.

In 1831, twenty-six-year-old Pleasant was tempted by the thousands of acres available in Texas for very little money. He came from a long line of pioneers of this frontier wilderness and had no fear of joining the migration west. Alone, Pleasant made an exploratory trip to Texas in 1831 or early 1832. He camped near a spring just north of the present site of the post office. While exploring, he found the Bedai tribe. He envisioned a future lucrative trade with them. He returned to Alabama to gather his family to the area. Pleasant was looking for land that looked like "home," and he found it in this "natural prairie in the middle of a vast forest with a pretty stream running nearby." He must have still been uncertain about moving his family, however, because he purchased a one hundred acre tract of land in Tennessee, "on the waters of Indian Creek" in December 1832.

Land grants in Texas were attractive to a frontiersman, but some native tribes were menacing. Dealings with the Mexican government were not always agreeable. Comanches and Apaches continually raided settlements, stealing horses and cattle from ranchers. After Mexico gained independence from Spain in 1821, Mexico needed settlers to defend the interior of Mexico from the Comanche raids. For this reason, they allowed Anglo immigration.

The government tried to control the flow of colonists by issuing land grants through the empresario system. Individuals such as Stephen F. Austin were granted vast tracts of land, which they were to issue as land grants to colonists who applied for permission to settle. Colonists were to meet certain requirements. They had to become Mexican citizens and declare loyalty to the Catholic faith. Mexico hoped to retain the territory with loyal and productive citizens in established communities. Thousands of land-hungry Americans immigrated to the "free land" of Texas. The new settlers displaced many tribes, intruding on their hunting grounds and creating further problems with the local tribes.

By September 1833, Pleasant had decided to move to Texas. He sold his land in Tennessee, and left Tipton County. Pleasant and Hannah settled on an empresario land grant near the spring he had originally discovered. The couple do not appear in the 1840 U.S. Census. Pleasant Gray received his legal grant of one league of seven square miles or about 4,428 acres in July of 1835. His grant came from Empresario José "Joseph" Vehlein. On November 20, 1834, Pleasant petitioned Vehlein in the proper Spanish format.

I, Pleasant Gray, a native of the United States of the North. . . Present myself before your Honor and say that attracted by the generous laws of colonization of this State, have come with my wife and three children to locate in it, if your Honor sees fit in view of the subjoined certificate to admit me as a colonist granting to me the corresponding quantity of land out of the vacant ones of the said enterprise. Wherefore I pray your Honor to please grant me the favor which I ask, for which favor I will live forever grateful.

Vehlein's attorney, A. Hotchkiss, instructed Land Commissioner Jorge Antonio Nixon to execute the order of survey. On November 24, 1834, Nixon decreed that Radford Berry would examine and translate the field notes, based on natural features of the land. The field notes describe Pleasant Gray's land as:

". . . thence west measured one thousand seven hundred varas [a Spanish measurement of approximately one yard] and . . . From which a white oak 12 inches in diameter bears south 69 degrees east 5-4/10 varas distant, and another white oak 12 inches in diameter bears south 51 degrees east; 7-2/10 varas distant, thence north measured two thousand one hundred varas . . . from which a wild china [Chinaberry tree] 14 inches in diameter bears north 39 degrees west . . . and a black walnut 8 inches in diameter bears south . . ."

Nixon then decreed on July 10, 1835, that the land was surveyed with two maps and a title in possession was issued as the P. Gray League:

Whereas Pleasant Gray has been received as a colonist in the Colonization enterprise contracted by Empresario Citizen José Vehlein, with the Supreme Government of the State, dated December 21, 1826, and the said Pleasant Gray having fully Proven that he is married, his family consisting of four persons, and finding in him requirements provided by the Law of Colonization of March 24, 1825, . . . I give, grant, and confer to the said Pleasant Gray, real and personal possession one league of land . . . whose bounds are on the map and field notes . . .the said land two labors [one labor is 177 acres] belong to the arable class and the balance to pasture . . . he being warned that within one year he must construct fixed and permanent land marks at every corner of the land, that he must settle upon and cultivate it in conformity with the provisions of said law . . ."

Pleasant Gray, his family, and his brother Ephraim, with his wife, arrived in the Huntsville area in 1835 with no settlements to welcome them. Pleasant built a small trading post near the spring he had discovered earlier. This spring is referred to as "never failing" in Huntsville histories. Henry Estill writes in his history of Huntsville:

On this tract they [Pleasant and Ephraim] pitched their camp near a cold spring of pure water, a few yards distant from the edge of a small prairie that lay like an oasis in the vast forest around it. Attracted by the beauty of the spot, and influenced by the fact that the spring was a favorite rendezvous for the peaceful Indians of the neighborhood, the Grays decided to establish here a trading post and build their home. Two cabins were soon erected from the logs of the forest, and a thriving trade sprang up with the neighboring Bedais and Coshatties [Coushattas] and occasional passing immigrants. As white Settlers began to occupy the surrounding country, the trading post developed into a store, the commodious log-cabin home into an inn . . ."

Estill identifies this "open prairie" as the present location of the public square and that the trading post was located on the east edge of the prairie. Pleasant and Hannah built a lumber home on the spot where W. H. Woodall's home was built (across Sam Houston Avenue from the First Methodist Church). Mr. Woodall's house contained some of the timbers of the original cabin. Ephraim Gray's house was built in "the cedars" near what is now the southeast corner of University Avenue and Tenth Street.

The settlement was divided into blocks covering an area of one square mile. The streets were named, from north to south: Milam,

Fannin, Cedar, Spring, Lamar, and Tyler. From east to west, they were Travis, Burton, Main, Jackson, Bell, and Farris.

The Gray family Bible lists Oliver Gray as being born on October 25, 1835, but in Pleasant's formal land requests to the Mexican Land Commissioner, dated November 1834, he declared that he had three children, which was a requirement to receive a legal land grant from Mexico.

Huntsville historians claim that David Crockett Gray, born on February 6, 1838, was the first Anglo child born in the Huntsville area. If there were no other children born in this area from 1834 to 1838, then the settlement of Pleasant and Ephraim Gray must have been very isolated.

The citizenship of the Gray children provides an interesting study of the changing control over Texas. Michael and David were United States citizens, having been born in Tennessee. Oliver was a Mexican citizen, born in Texas before the revolution of 1836. David was born a citizen of the Republic of Texas in 1838. Their sisters, Amanda Texanna and Mary Frances "Mollie" born in 1841 and 1843 respectively, were also born in the republic of Texas. Hannah Elizabeth "Bettie" was born in 1846, a citizen of the United States after Texas became a state in the Union in 1845.

Pleasant Gray's trading post and Ephraim Gray's general store were very successful. Pleasant bartered for goods with the Bedai, who lived on Bedais Creek where it empties into the Trinity River, as well as with the Alabama-Coushatta, the Neches, the Nacogdoches, and other small tribes. The natives brought bear fat and skins, deer and small animal pelts, herbs, pecans and hickory nuts, and corn to trade for mustang ponies and robes brought by other tribes from the plains, and fish and seashells from the coastal tribes. They also made baskets, bags, and sandals of yucca plant fibers to sell at the trading post.

The dreaded Comanche were known to raid as far south as San Antonio. The peaceful Cherokee settled north of Huntsville and provided a barrier against the hostile tribes. Huntsville was also located on the edge of the Big Thicket, and the Comanche seldom raided settlements in the forested areas.

Ephraim received goods for his store "by wagon from Houston or by boat from Cincinnati [a Texas town north of Huntsville on the Trinity River] thence by wagon to Huntsville." The pioneer settlers of Huntsville lived simply. Fish could be found in the creeks, vegetables were planted in small plots, and men could hunt squirrels, deer, and wild turkeys in the woods. Grazing land was plentiful for the livestock.

Pleasant and Ephraim served a rural, farming community of timber and cotton plantations. The Gibbs Brothers, also early settlers, arrived in 1841 and built a mercantile on the new town square. In 1848, after Texas became a state, Sam and Margaret Houston built their Woodland Home on a 200-acre plantation in Huntsville.

The settlement remained small. After ten years, the population was only about one hundred citizens in the mid-1840s. Under the new Republic of Texas, Huntsville was formally established and named by Pleasant Gray for his home in Alabama. The town was located in Washington County, which later divided into smaller counties. Montgomery County, which extended north to include the town of Huntsville, was created in 1837. After Texas was admitted to the Union as a state, Walker County was separated and formed a new county in 1847, in honor of Robert J. Walker, a Senator from Mississippi who introduced the resolution in the United States Senate recognizing the independence of Texas. In 1860, the county was renamed Samuel H. Walker County in honor of the Texas Ranger, as a protest when Robert J. Walker refused to support the Confederacy.

Pleasant and Hannah deeded "for one cent consideration" and his "regard for the health prosperity, and success of the people and its vicinity, a parcel of 50,265 square feet of land in Huntsville, for the use of the public and for building a courthouse thereon [known in the plan of the town as the Public Square] bounded on the north, east, south, and west by Cedar [Eleventh] Street, Main [University

Avenue], Spring [Twelfth] Street, and Jackson [Sam Houston] Avenue respectively. The town's population had grown to about 500 by 1849.

The "Brick Academy," formally known as the "Huntsville Academy," was the first official school established in Huntsville. It was built on a five-acre tract of land donated by Pleasant and Hannah Gray in 1841, land that is now within the Huntsville Prison Walls Unit. The Baptist church held the first church services in the "Brick Academy" during the early years of the settlement. The school became the Female Academy in 1843, and the Grays donated more land to Huntsville Trustees for the academy, which was incorporated in 1846.

Pleasant involved himself in land development and sales. He built a frame house in 1841 called the Globe Tavern, located just north of the present location of the *Huntsville Item* office. The inn was a favorite rest stop for travelers and was sold to the Woodall family in 1853.

Pleasant built and leased several other buildings, one of which was a mercantile run by Thomas Gibbs and Gardner Coffin, rented for a fee of two dollars and fifty cents per month. Pleasant Gray also bought land for others. His 1849 tax receipt indicates that he represented Thomas Scott in the procurement of 640 acres in Montgomery County in 1841.

Pleasant bartered land for goods and possessions that he and his family wanted. He traded 184 acres of land, valued at $600, to Francis L. Hatch of Huntsville for a female slave named Kesiah to be a servant for Hannah. Hannah kept this bill of sale in her family Bible. When the Gray family set out to relocate to California in 1856, Hannah was not able to take Kesiah because California was a free state. Kesiah was probably sold before the family left Texas.

Pleasant and Hannah also sold a parcel of land in 1845 to their eldest son Michael for the price of $200, "described on a map of said town of Huntsville as lot Number 36 in block number two, commencing on Jackson Street and running west 150 feet . . ."

In 1847, for the sum of one dollar, Pleasant Gray provided land for "the purpose of a place of burial free to all persons and for no other purpose," which is now Oakwood Cemetery. Milam Street [Ninth] fronted the plot and extended to Travis Street [Avenue I] on one side and Houston Street [Avenue H] on the other side." The original tract has been enlarged. The eastern side was designated for people of color, and many slaves were buried there. Pleasant Gray also sold ninety-four acres to the State of Texas in 1846 for the purpose of building a penitentiary. Grace McGary and Rover Smither provided land to join Pleasant Gray's section for a total selling price of $493. The prison logged only three prisoners in 1849.

Pleasant Gray lived in Texas from 1834 to 1849. Upon news of the gold rush in California, he decided to explore and prospect in California. He was well established in Huntsville, but he was described as a "plain unlettered pioneer . . . with a more than ordinary degree of enterprise." Pleasant traveled to St. Louis, Missouri to join the Santa Fe Trail. Don Reid, Jr. writes in the "Bicentennial History" about a local tale explaining Pleasant Gray's demise.

"Gray tried to buy a strikingly beautiful horse from an Indian chief Who lived nearby, but the chief refused to sell. A short time later Gray left for California on the horse, telling friends that the Indian had finally agreed to sell the horse to him. Soon afterwards, the chief was found in the forest, murdered. In a few weeks, residents of Walker County heard that Pleasant Gray had died of a strange illness. But the old-timers said that the Indians had tracked Gray and killed him for they believed that he had killed their chief."

A copy of Pleasant Gray's will was found in the family Bible.

"I, Pleasant Gray, of said state and county, being of sound mind and on the eve of my departure for California and being sensible of the uncertainty of human life and desirous of making a just and equitable division of my estate, do make and ordain this my last will and testament in manner and form following. I give, decree and bequeath to my beloved wife, Hannah Gray, after all my just debts have been paid during her natural life, all my estate, real, personal, and mixed to use the profits, products, and increase

thereof, for the purpose of supporting and educating my children; and with the power to sell any portion of my lands and Negroes for the purpose of educating my children, but for no other purpose.

I give decree and bequeath after the death of my said wife, Hannah Gray, to my children as follows: To my son Michael Gray, an equal portion of my estate after deducting from his portion six hundred dollars, which amount he has received out of my estate. To my son, John A.W. Gray, an equal portion; to my son, Oliver H. gray, an equal portion; to my son, David Crockett Gray, an equal portion; to my daughter, Elizabeth Hannah an equal portion; and I make and constitute my wife, Hannah Gray, my executrix in this my last will and testament, and exempt her from giving bond as executrix, with full power and authority to execute and carry out the premises of the forgoing will. In testimony whereof I, the said Pleasant Gray, after reading of the foregoing, will have hereto signed my name at Huntsville in said County and State aforesaid, this thirteenth day of March One thousand eight hundred and forty-nine.

With Pleasant Gray's will, Hannah always kept her receipts and important records in the family bible. A tax bill dated September 20, 1849, lists a total of 1,216 acres, nineteen town lots, and an unstated number of slaves. Also found in the family bible are documents showing that Michael and John Gray petitioned the court of Walker County in March of 1852 to declare the will of Pleasant Gray null and void. They felt that they were deprived of their due inheritance because they could not receive any property until after the death of their mother, Hannah Gray, which might not occur in their lifetimes. The will was not overturned, but this disagreement did not appear to have harmed the family relationships.

Michael soon followed Pleasant's trail to California. His name appears in the California Census of 1850. He became a sheriff and tax collector in Yuba County, California, and later settled in Tombstone, Arizona. He returned to Huntsville in 1856 to settle his affairs with the will petition, and to help Hannah and the younger children prepare for their move to California. Hannah remarried in California in 1858.

There are no records indicating whether Ephraim Gray remained in Huntsville or if he relocated elsewhere.

A paper entitled *Phrenological Chart of Pleasant Gray by John Wesley Woodward, The Deaf Mute, June 2, 1847,* was found among the other papers in the Gray family Bible. Quotations of it read:

> *You are honest as regards debts, money, and would act on the square in that respect, but let any man who is not a Mason look out if he has a pretty wife. You love children, yet will pet them one moment and curse them the next. You are passionate, ardent, decided, prompt, and self-willed . . . Coaxed a little and humored you are pleasant and mildly spoken, but taken across the grain you are awfully rough . . . You can lie when in a tight place though your general disposition is to speak too plainly and openly. You make many enemies by not keeping your mouth shut. You have traveled and had a disposition to do so, can shut up your eyes and form a perfect map in your mind of places you were once in . . . Your great fault is that you do things in too great a hurry and with too great vehemence.*
>
> *God help your wife . . . she will have to wear the petticoats and keep small broomsticks. Your character is not amiable, but it is warm, passionate, just, and generous.*

These were times of tumult, independence, rebirth, and adventure in Texas. Natives, wars, and political controversies surrounded Pleasant Gray, but his small trading post settlement was not directly involved or harmed by misfortune. With his generous donations of land to establish the town square, cemetery, and schools, Pleasant Gray set in motion a time-honored tradition of progressive educational, political, and cultural activity in the community of Huntsville.

CHAPTER 8

The Early Churches of Huntsville

By David Parnell

The Farris family, who built the small chapel at the community of Goshen on the West Sandy, and the Gray family of Huntsville, were part of a growing and determined group of Christians who settled in Walker County during the early 1830s and 1840s. Many of the early settlers sought religious solace in their homes.

For those who arrived in Texas prior to 1836, under the government of Mexico, Catholicism was the state religion, and none of the early Protestant faiths could worship legally. Although church meetings were illegal, the Mexican government did not stop families from meeting for bible studies in each other's homes.

It was not until 1836 and the independence of Texas that the various Protestant denominations began to found churches in Texas. The lack of money and limited agricultural economy prevented many of the devoted Christians from carrying out their desires to build churches. It was not a lack of desire, but a lack of funds that prevented the construction of early churches. One devoted missionary woman disagreed. In her book, *Texas in 1850*, Melinda Rankin wrote:

> *The prospective importance of Huntsville naturally suggests the inquiry, are the religious interests to keep pace with the progress of other*

departments of improvements? Will the Christian, alone, remain inactive in the midst of such a toiling, parting generation?

In the haste of citizens of Huntsville to build the town with public buildings, churches have been, evidently, overlooked. The building of churches seems to have been of minor importance. The honor of the town demands that it should possess this defining mark of worship to Almighty God.

Due to the present lack of numbers of the different religious groups, No single one has been strong enough to build a church by itself.

Those who profess to be Christians contain all various groups, but Each denomination is considered few and feeble.

THE METHODIST CHURCH

Methodists had already begun to organize conferences attended by both ministers and laymen. They expanded their meetings into Texas after Texas independence in 1836. The first church or congregation of Methodists in the Huntsville area dates from the early 1830s and was located about eight miles southwest of Huntsville near what is now known as Johnson's Chapel, formerly Martha's Chapel.

In 1843, the fourth Texas Methodist Conference meeting was held in the Robinson settlement, a few miles below the present town of Huntsville. Deed records show that the Methodists purchased a lot in Huntsville which measured one hundred by 150 feet, fronting on Jackson Street from Isaac McGary for $500. The deed was dated August 26, 1854.

The first Methodist church building was erected in 1857, with the Reverend A. Davis as pastor. Reverend Robert Alexander gave the dedication sermon. In 1888, this building was torn down and replaced by a larger one on the same site. A large wooden structure was added, which served as a Sunday School for the younger classes. This new addition was built about 1900. In 1910, a fire destroyed this wooden structure and damaged the main auditorium and the pipe organ. The reverend E. W. Solomon began a movement for a new and larger building. This project was completed in 1912, but six years later this building was also destroyed by fire. In 1919, the present church was reconstructed. Thus, there have been four houses of worship on this site.

Few records are available about the work of the women of the Church. Their service was particularly notable in Sunday School, in various women's organizations, and in social activities. At times, the ladies have been solely responsible for much of the finances. This was true in the earlier years, when the pastor's salary partly depended upon church suppers and similar money-raising affairs.

THE PRESBYTERIANS

The Cumberland Presbyterian Church was the first group to erect a church building in Huntsville. The Reverand Weyman Adair established the church at a very early date in the history of the city and was its first pastor. In 1850, the contract for the first church building in the town was let by the Cumberland Presbyterians. Misfortune befell the congregation, and during the Civil War its membership declined. The church was finally disbanded in 1886. The remaining members joined other congregations in the city.

The First Presbyterian Church of Texas, although similar in many of their beliefs to the Cumberland Presbyterians, maintained a separate church hierarchy. In 1843, the Texas Synod of the Presbyterian Church contained three presbyteries: Texas, Red River, and Colorado. In 1845, a fourth presbytery, Trinity, was added. In 1848, the Texas Synod requested the general assembly to shift the boundaries once again and expanded to the Presbytery of the Brazos, which included Huntsville. Among the early Presbyterians were Josiah H. Bell and his wife, Mary Evelyn, who had crossed the Sabine on April 22, 1821, on their way to Huntsville.

In June 1848, the congregation of Huntsville's First Presbyterian Church was organized by the Presbytery of Brazos, with Reverend P. H. Fullenwider as moderator. Before their first building was erected, services were held in the courthouse, in the Cumberland Presbyterian Church building and in the chapel of Austin College. The church members bought a lot in 1855, and the First Presbyterian Church building was erected in 1856. This building was used until a new church was constructed on the same site. In 1856, the third church was built in a new location on the southwest corner of Avenue R and Nineteenth Streets.

The Presbyterian Church became actively involved in the community of Huntsville. In 1849, the Brazos Presbytery of the Old School Presbyterian Church decided to create a college. The college was located in Huntsville the following year. The college went into operation in 1852 with Dr. Daniel Baker as its first president. The founders first considered naming the school San Jacinto College, but finally chose Austin College in honor of Stephen F. Austin.

THE BAPTIST CHURCH

On September 16, 1844, the First Baptist Church of Huntsville was organized under its first pastor, Z. N. Morrell. The first organizational meeting of the Baptist church took place in the Brick Academy Building located on a five-acre tract fronting on Twelfth Street and Avenue G. Reverend Z. N. Morrell described holding services in the summer months before the formal organization of the church in a "little log house." Beginning in 1838, the Dean School was a wooden building used by another group of Baptists. The congregation of the Huntsville Baptist Church occasionally used the building for their services as well.

In 1851, R. C. Burleson, President of Baylor University, preached the sermon at the dedication of the First Baptist Church building. This was not Dr. Burleson's first visit to Huntsville. He had held a meeting in the town in October of 1848. Among those present at the dedication were General Sam Houston and his wife who joined all of the members present to come to the altar at the end of the service and reconsecrate themselves to God. In its early years, even after the construction of the first building, the members of the Baptist Church sometimes met at Dean's school. Baptisms were held at a creek near Dean's school and at the pool near Sam Houston's home. It may have been in the pool near Houston's home where he was said to have jokingly remarked that if his sins had been washed away, he felt sorry for the fish.

The Baptist Church began with eight members, but by 1896 the church had reached an enrollment of 144 members. The General and Mrs. Margaret Houston joined the church on December 16, 1855. The General participated in local church meetings and committees and was named a delegate to the 1856 and 1858 Baptist State Convention. The Houstons and two of their servants received Letters of Dismission from the Huntsville Church on July 16, 1859.

In 1850, Melinda Parker reported that the Baptists were the most numerous church-goers in Huntsville and that the church had prospered because the economic conditions had been very good. In 1872, Pastor Z. N. Morrell maintained that the Baptist Church of Huntsville was the oldest in middle Texas.

The Second Baptist Church building, dedicated in 1891, remained in use until 1924. This building was demolished in order to provide for a newer and larger building. The third building burned in 1954 and on December 11, 1955, the fourth and current building was dedicated.

THE FIRST CHRISTIAN CHURCH

Mr. J. W. Bush, a member of the Church of God begun by Alexander Campbell of Kentucky arrived in Huntsville in December 1853. The following year, he helped establish the Church of God (Christian) on

January 1, 1854, in Huntsville. The early members met in the courthouse and in homes of private families for worship, continuing to meet in this manner until 1857 or 1858. The first resident pastor of the Huntsville church arrived on January 1, 1863. Seventeen members formed the congregation at that time, but the church membership grew rapidly. During the Civil War, a few devout Black families were baptized members and attended services regularly.

The first building used by the Church of God was bought from the local Cumberland Presbyterians about 1868. A new building was constructed on the same lot, the Northwest corner of Avenue J and Eleventh Street in 1901. It served as a place of worship until 1931, when another Church of God was dedicated.

ST. STEPHENS EPISCOPAL CHURCH

The Episcopalians arrived in Texas after most of the major denominations were already established and after Texas had become a state. On May 9, 1850, as the first annual convention of the Diocese in Houston, Episcopal Bishop Freeman appointed a general missionary to travel about the state. He was to look into promising situations and officiate in places wherever members of the church were found. He also proposed a diocesan school for educating young men for the ministry. After the next years' convention, in 1851, the church members built a school at Anderson.

St. Stephen's Church is the sixth oldest in the Episcopal Diocese of Texas and counts among the oldest churches in Huntsville. Before the construction of St. Stephen's, the congregation met in the Cumberland Presbyterian Church building, in the Oddfellows Hall, and the upper room of the courthouse. Nathaniel Charlot, the first ordained Episcopal priest in the area, was appointed missionary for Cold Spring and Huntsville on January 2, 1859. H felt that Huntsville had more potential than Cold Spring, and eventually settled in Huntsville in 1872. By the end of the Civil War, the post-war depression prevented the church members from building a church and they had to continue meeting in the Courthouse. It was not until March 23, 1873, that Bishop Gregg consecrated the first St. Stephen's Episcopal Church.

RELIGION IN HUNTSVILLE

Since the foundation of the early churches of Huntsville, many denominations and churches have developed. Church membership has increased for all of the various Protestant and Catholic faiths. The religious life of Huntsville has continued to grow. Church members are credited with much of the care for indigents and elderly over the years. All of the churches have remained involved in church gatherings to raise money for community projects. Church members have continued to take an interest in the growth of Huntsville and in the spread of Christian beliefs in the region. Most churches also sponsor missions and support missionaries throughout the world. The early growth of Christian churches in Huntsville is an indication of the continuing interest of Huntsville in its church life.

CHAPTER 9

Social History of the Farris-Roberts Cabin

By Ross Lovell, Ph.D.

To appreciate the life of early settlers in the Farris-Roberts Cabin, we need to place it in its social context in the early 1840s in East Texas. The people who migrated to Texas from the United States usually came in groups of family and friends. Once these families became established, they would invite other family and friends to join them in Texas. Parts of Texas were dominated by immigrants from the same states. East Texas was primarily settled by immigrants from Tennessee and Alabama. They brought with them the Southern culture of their native states.

Like so many, Hezekiah Farris moved to East Texas in 1835 from Tennessee. He came with his brothers William and Richard, and they settled their families near each other on a 640-acre headright in what was then Montgomery County. Allen Roberts, son of Hezekiah's wife Matilda from her first marriage, moved to Texas in 1837 and settled next to his mother and stepfather.

The majority of settlers in East Texas in the early 1840s lived in log cabins. These log cabins had two common floor plans: a single room cabin, usually about eighteen feet square, and a two-room cabin separated by a covered space called a dog run. The cheapest and easiest of these cabins to build had a single room made of unfinished logs. These could be easily erected by amateur laborers. Once the pine or oak trees were felled, a task which might take months for the landowner, the cabins could be built in two days by men at a cost of approximately twenty dollars. A two- room cabin with a dog run made of hewn pine logs required three men three days to finish at a cost of about seventy-five dollars, as long as the logs were already cut and hewn.

Most cabins were built by semiprofessional carpenters working for hire. Often these carpenters were black slaves who were rented to neighbors for the duration of the house-raising. Usually, cabins in east Texas were made of pine or oak which were the most available material. The Farris-Roberts cabin was a single room approximately eighteen feet square. It is built of hewn logs which indicates that skilled builders built the cabin. It could be that Allen Roberts' stepfather helped provide him with the skilled labor.

Log cabins were primarily furnished with homemade furniture. Even in well-to-do houses few luxuries could be found since transporting prized furnishings from Tennessee or Alabama was difficult and oftentimes impossible, if the family came on foot or by ship. The problem primarily stemmed from inadequate transportation. East Texas was isolated from the Texas trade centers and markets. There were few navigable rivers, and bad roads were common. There were some craftsmen and carpenters that could make furniture from native woods, but these were in short supply.

The clothes worn by most of the settlers were homespun garments made by the women, who spent much of their time spinning and weaving. Men often wore buckskin shirts and moccasins with homespun trousers. The cost of clothing and food can be seen from a case file Number 23 of Walker/Montgomery County Clerk documents. This case shows cost for board and lodging for a family of four paid by the court from their father's estate.

Listed among the food items are:

1 lb. Coffee	20 cents
1 chicken	25 cents
1 lb. cheese	20 cents

1 lb. salt	10 cents
14 lbs. sugar	$2.00
1 steer for slaughtering	$10.00

Clothing and other necessities were listed:

1 umbrella	$2.00
2 dozen shirt buttons	20 cents
1 pair suspenders	45 cents
1 bar soap	15 cents
1 pair boots	$3.00
1 pair shoes	$1.25
1 pair blankets	$9.00
Gallon of whiskey	$2.00
1 clock	$20.00
Feeding 1 horse for 5 months	$20.00
Feeding 1 yoke of oxen	$20.00

The rural farmers in East Texas fell into two classes. The yeoman farmer worked his farm by himself with his family members. The purpose of this farm was to provide subsistence for the family and then some type of cash crop, either cotton or corn. The small planter had five to twenty slaves, and a large number of acres planted in cotton.

All farmers shared the problem of getting their crops to market. Agents from Galveston, Sabine Pass, or New Orleans mercantile houses commonly bought the farmers' crops. It was the farmers' problem to deliver the crops to the coastal merchants, who paid only upon receipt.

Farmers often needed loans to tide them over until the sale of the crops. In the early 1840s there were no banks in what is now Walker County. Loans were primarily provided by Huntsville merchants. Promissory notes were used to record these transactions. Ten percent interest seemed to be the standard interest rate. Promissory notes were often written on scraps of paper, but always included a reliable witness. By the 1860s and the beginning of the Civil War, promissory notes were printed and often included illustrated artwork which might show the changes in travel. Instead of a sailing ship, there might be a steam train running on double tracks, or a steam ship. In Huntsville, General Francis L. Hatch, the editor of the local newspaper, *The Texas Banner*, printed promissory notes as well as official courthouse papers.

The City of Huntsville was incorporated in 1845 and provided products and services for the surrounding rural communities. The Globe Tavern, the first frame building in Huntsville, provided a local "watering hole" and a stop for stagecoaches traveling from Houston to Cincinnati, a shipping port on the Trinity River. The tavern also provided entertainment for the community. Bishop Morris, travelling through Texas in 1841, recounts "citizens of the town collected at the Tavern to enjoy the pitiful entertainment of hearing a trifling fellow pat his foot and draw his fiddle bow to kill time and chase dullness from the city."

Two mercantiles were available. The Gibbs-Coffin and the Alexander McDonald's. These stores provided supplies for the rural area. Two days away by horse or wagon, there was a sawmill operated by William Viser which provided lumber for buildings in Huntsville and the surrounding area. *The Texas Banner*, the local weekly newspaper, provided local news and advertising. Weekly mail service was available from Houston to Huntsville. The city of Huntsville had a Masonic Lodge which met above McDonald's store.

Transportation was difficult in early Texas. Floods often washed out crossings and roads. A coach, which arrived with the mail and passengers, came through once a week from Cincinnati on its way to Houston, unless bad weather or floods prevented travel. The stagecoaches were carefully protected from damage since they were expensive, valued at $200. Horses cost one hundred dollars to $150 each.

Stagecoach owners might contract with the United States government to carry the mail and offered passenger service as a bonus. The coaches might also carry bulk items such as government revenue or tax stamps which were used on mortgages and deeds for the sale of land, and blanks for telegrams.

Postal deliveries were made in Huntsville as early as 1839. The route came from Houston, through Huntsville, and on to Cincinnati, a major port on the Trinity River. There were no stamps yet, but the amount of postage due was written on the envelope by the receiving post office. The letter carrier collected the amount due at the destination and marked the envelope "paid" as he handed it over to the addressee. Since letters were uncommon, people often treasured letters, saving them to hand down to their descendants.

Schooling was provided by a male academy. Students boarded in town and attended the Brick Academy. Only later did the school provide education to both young men and women in the surrounding area.

Most of the social life in the county was provided by community churches. The Farris Methodist Chapel was a log cabin built around 1841. The people sat on benches made from split logs. The Chapel was used not only by Methodists, but by Presbyterians and Baptists. Robinson Settlement Camp Grounds, eight miles from Huntsville, had a spacious building of heavy pine logs and offered another place for church meetings.

The Huntsville Baptist Fellowship met in homes in Huntsville, as did the Methodist Fellowship. Church was usually an all-day affair because of the long distances people had to travel to attend church services. The gathered congregation sang hymns; the preacher preached; families ate their picnic lunches on the grounds; children played; women gossiped; and men discussed politics, the weather, and farm crops.

Weddings and Christmas provided the best opportunities for friends and neighbors to get together and socialize. William Bollaert described a wedding that he attended in the vicinity of Huntsville in 1843. He said friends and neighbors traveled to the bride's house and by nightfall, between 150 and 200 persons had congregated, including men, women, boys, girls, and babies. The women in the bride's party were all dressed in white. The bridegroom rode up on horseback escorted by a squadron of his best friends. The minister commenced the marriage ceremony and once the man and wife were legally wed, supper was announced. After supper, there was music with fiddle playing and singing. About midnight older people and women with babies began the trip back home with their slaves going ahead with a fire pan to light the way. The younger people who stayed behind danced, played games, and drank whiskey until the early morning. After a good breakfast, everyone left to return to their homes.

Mr. Bollaert gave us a description of a Christmas day in 1843. Hosts served eggnog in the morning, followed by neighbors visiting each other. Everyone joined in the dinner and merrymaking in the evening. Gifts for the children were usually homemade toys such as corn cob dolls for the girls and wood-carved animals for the boys. There were no Christmas trees since that was not yet part of the Christmas scene. Candy pulling was a game that young and old played at Christmas time. Molasses was boiled down until thick, then couples would take turns stretching or pulling the candy, wrapping it over itself and pulling again until the candy hardened. Dances and music were always a part of the evening revelry. Quadrilles, contra dancing, and reels were the popular dances.

During Christmas time, slaves were given a week's holiday. They decked out in their best clothes and visited together with singing and dancing. Bolleart described a Christmas Ball held in Mr. McDonald's unfinished store in Huntsville. The Ball was orderly, with dancing and singing and a supper at midnight. At daylight they returned to their respective homes. Their Christmas holiday was over.

Injury and disease were also part of the life of East Texas settlers. The country doctor had to be physician, surgeon, and apothecary.

He often traveled many miles to visit patients. He was usually paid in cotton, pigs, cows, or other agricultural products. The cost for a doctor's services included night visits at one dollar per mile and a day visit at fifty cents per mile. Quinine was often prescribed since it was the standard medicine for malaria, a common disease throughout the Southern coastal regions, particularly in swamplands and river bottoms.

In Texas, malaria was called "ague" or simply "chills and fever." It was not a disease seen often in Huntsville. Yellow fever, which was also spread by mosquitoes, had decimated the population of the nearby town of Cincinnati in 1853. An epidemic of yellow fever struck Huntsville in 1867, although there was not a large mosquito population. Many years later, as timber was cleared, and cattle tanks were built in pastures, mosquitoes increased to more dangerous levels.

Doctors did the best they could with the information they had to diagnose diseases common in the area, but they had few weapons to battle the many ailments which they faced. For fevers, doctors practiced "cupping," a technique in which a heated glass was placed against the skin. As a vacuum formed from the cooling air, the skin was sucked upwards into a blood blister. The blood was thought to help remove the disease.

A more dangerous medication was made from the roots of the "*scilla*," a flowering bulb. The bulb was boiled into a syrup and administered as a diuretic, or as an expectorant to reduce the phlegm in the throat and lungs. It also worked as a heart stimulant, although it could kill the patient if used in large enough quantities. An indication of its lethal effects was that it was also used as rat poison.

Funerals in frontier East Texas were handled by family and neighbors. The women prepared the body. The men dug the grave and built the coffin. The coffin was borne by relatives with neighbors following from the house to the grave site. The body was lowered into the grave, then friends or family recited memories of the deceased. A prayer followed and the family returned to the house with neighbors who closed the grave. The grave was either in a frontier cemetery such as the Farris Cemetery, or on family land. Hezekiah Farris donated land for a community cemetery in 1843, which was used by all of the families in the surrounding area.

Many of the social activities of early Texas took place in the Farris-Roberts cabin. The cabin's residents, in particular the Roberts and Farris families during the earliest years of settlement, experienced births and deaths, weddings and parties. There were Christmas gatherings and family socials and everyone shared in the frontier lifestyle. Illnesses were handled at home since Huntsville was too far for early doctors to make the long trip. Schools for children, until the twentieth century, had to be within one or two miles, walking distance for the children. Other children, who lived on distant farms, had to learn at home. Churches, like the Farris Chapel, were built within a wagon ride's distance. Since Sunday was usually the only day that families relaxed, church services, no matter how far, were an opportunity to gather and celebrate for the whole day.

By the turn of the century, when the Farris family had moved to a better home, sharecroppers took up residence in the cabin. They worked the Farris land, exchanging part of the crop which they produced for rental of the land and cabin. In the 1920s, the Farris family rented the land to tenant farmers who sold their own crops as best they could and paid for the use of the land. Neither sharecroppers nor tenant farmers ever made enough to live comfortably and spent much of their time hunting in the woods and fishing to provide sufficient food for their families.

An illness could wipe out a family's meager savings. Doctors from Huntsville may have visited the tenants, who would have paid in-kind. The payments might be crops from their small vegetable gardens, a few eggs from their chicken, or butter or cheese from the milk cow.

Family cabins were the center of social life. With the coming of the modern era, however, as families moved to modern, brick homes, with air conditioning and heat and indoor plumbing, many of the early families looked back on their lives in the cabins with disdain and contempt. The logs cabins were allowed to deteriorate. Termites and dry rot destroyed the lowest logs, which collapsed into dust heaps on the ground. Upper logs slowly crumbled and decayed until there was nothing left but the scraps of roof and termite dust. The stories of the social life of the people remained in the memories and the books, but the places where those happy and sad times took place were gone. Only a few people such as the Farris family have thought to preserve what they can of the past social life of their ancestors.

CHAPTER 10

Adventures on the Land

The Human Impact on Farris Land in Western Walker County

By Randy White

Environmental historians focus on man's interaction and interrelationship with the land to explain historical developments, how man has impacted the land, animals, and plants in his environment. The American West has been one of the main areas of study for environmental historians, building the distinctiveness of the region first enunciated by Texan historian Waler Prescott Webb. Works such as Andrew C. Isenberg's *The Destruction of the Bison: An Environmental History, 1750-1920* touch on areas of Texas. Much more work remains to be done to generate a more complete picture of Texas's environmental past.

We add to the growing body of knowledge by studying the Farris family lands in western Walker County, Texas. The land is part of the Coastal Plain that stretches across the southern United States. Long before Hezekiah Farris received his initial grant, plants and animals populated the area. Later, Native Americans moved across the land. The most recent of these were the Bedai or Bedais Natives, an agricultural hunter-gatherer people. Most recently, Euro Americans arrived.

The greatest changes, and the ones most easily recognizable, resulted from the actions of farmers and agriculturalists who settled on and used the land for farming and cattle raising. Some of the results of their activities remain, while parts of the land appear nearly undisturbed.

Most of southeastern Texas is made up of clay soils. The Farris lands are no exception. A federal soil survey of Walker County in the late 1970s revealed that the Farris land was nearly all clay. The land consists of rolling hills with gentle slopes, underlain by deep clays that hold varying levels of acidity. The soil has never been very amenable to agriculture. Few plants thrive in it. Pines, mainly loblolly pine, shortleaf pine, and slash pine grow adequately well, as do hard woods such as hack berry, water oak, willow oak, green ash, and elm. The land can also support grasses such as common Bermuda grass, coastal Bermuda grass, lespedeza, and burl clover. Other plants which the land could support were butter willows, rushes, and the ubiquitous Johnson grass. Unfortunately for the agriculturalist, the land had marginal to low potential for cultivated crops such as cotton.

Along with the limited potential as a course of agricultural exploitation, the clays on the Farris property, both sloping and in the bottomlands, tended to prevent water from reaching the roots of the plants by keeping the water on the surface. These heavy clays "keep water from the plants." No matter how much the Tennessee and Alabama farmers cleared the land, there was a natural limit to what it could produce. The soil generally had limited permeability and drained very slowly. Water tended to stay on the surface after heavy rainfalls, some of it for up to two weeks. While "total annual precipitation is normally adequate for cotton, feed grains, and small grains," the water trapped on top of the soils hampered agriculture. Further, the soil survey found the inability of the native soils to bear intense cultivation because "most soil required extensive fertilizer application to be brought into production." This land would not be very suitable for agricultural development brought by the Euroamericans. It did, however, support a population of deer, bear, bison, and bobcats along with various species of birds.

It was probably the pursuit of these animals that drew the first Native Americans to Walker County. Exactly how many different groups crossed the county, and the Farris lands, will never be known. The last group of free-roaming Natives to live on the land were the Bedais. A Bedais village was located on West Sandy Creek, just below the final location of the log cabin. Virtually nothing is known about this particular band, other than their location on the West Sandy and a few arrowheads discovered by the Farris children over the years.

Scholars have studied the Bedais as a people. This band undoubtedly lived in much the same way as other Bedais tribes. The Bedais were an agricultural people, culturally very similar to the Caddo. Available information indicates the Bedais were "good deer hunters who planted and reaped good crops of corn, and were honest and peaceful." The Bedais must have farmed corn as well as hunted deer to augment their diet and made hunting trips for the bison roaming nearby. The Bedais early farming must have impacted the land as they cleared land for their crops and village. Small-scale subsistence farming has little impact on the land, but what the Bedais started would be greatly expanded by Hezekiah Farris and his descendants.

When Hezekiah Farris received his grant of land in the newly created Washington County, (later Montgomery and finally Walker County) the land was fairly pristine. Cotton was king in the pre-Civil War south, and cotton was the only cash crop Hezekiah could raise. The Farris family cotton was ginned at Shiro. The family also had a garden for vegetables, such as peas, sweet corn, and corn for their cows.

Cattle raising on the Farris land has always been limited by the available pasturage. The cotton which Hezekiah introduced depleted the already limited nutrients in the land, since cotton is very taxing on the soil. The addition of cattle further damaged the soil as the cattle trampled on the land and depleted the ground cover. The following two generations, James Morgan Farris and James Hezekiah Farris, both continued to plant cotton and raise cattle.

The Farris family faced the constant problem of clay soils. Rainfall would rush down the slopes, settling in the in the lower areas, creating bogs and swamps. The Farris' compensated by terracing the slopes to grow more cotton. Even with the alterations, the poor soil conditions hampered the productivity of good crops.

The family even tried growing various nuts and fruits. They planted pecan, apple, plum, peach, and walnut groves. They even took advantage of the indigenous grapes. The Farris family worked the land by standard methods of the time, replacing the native plant life with European crops and restocking the land with cattle. The cattle eliminated the forage available for the deer, and as frontier families hunted the local deer and bear for food, the once plentiful herds were eventually depleted.

The Farris family worked the land more intensely than the Bedais, but had not used pesticides or fertilizers other than cow manure. They used walnut trees to control pests like ticks. Extensive use of pesticides and insecticides were not in general use until the years after World War II.

The Farris lands, like much of Walker County, were originally covered with timber. During the early years of the 20th century, timber companies such as the Kirby Lumber Company, began harvesting the forests of East Texas, seeing them as a renewable resource. In order to help with family finances during the 1920s and 30s, Alton Farris sold off most of the old-growth forest on the Farris family land to the timber companies. With little profit from cotton, he went to work for a timber company and worked to help cut down the remaining old growth forests until a chainsaw accident nearly took off one of his thumbs.

The result for Walker County was the removal of what remained of the old forests. Today's trees, which include those on the Farris property and on the National Forest lands, are all second growth. Still visible, however, are the remnants of old fruit and nut groves.

Alton Farris, unaware of the ecological implications of his actions, took other measures to alter the family lands. Natural springs and wetlands covered part of his holdings. In the late 1940s and early 1950s, he removed the wetlands as a problem by dynamite and bulldozing. He dug holes along the edges of the swamp and dropped in dynamite. He also bulldozed whole sections of the swampy areas. The resulting loss of wetlands would have been illegal thirty years later. Neighbors also affected the Farris land. Several sank wells, draining the local water table. The drop in the water table dried up many of the Farris springs.

CONCLUSION

The use by humans of what we know as the Farris lands generally reflects the prevailing trends of the last century. The Bedais were agriculturalists and grew subsistence crops on the land while hunting the available game. Hezekiah Farris and his immediate descendants altered the land and brought in domesticated and exotic plants and animals. These changes sent the native populations into decline. Subsequent generations took advantage of newer technology to further change the land from its natural state in order to make a living from the land. The land, however, had limited potential for crop production.

All land cannot remain a wilderness. The first efforts at environmental conservation begun by President Theodore Roosevelt at the beginning of the twentieth century created many wilderness areas for the benefit of future generations. The concept of preservation of wilderness has long included an argument that some wilderness should be set aside for human use. Such utilitarian use of the land can be read into the debates surrounding the creation of national wilderness lands in the Sam Houston National Forest abutting the current Farris lands. Representative Bob Eckhardt of Houston introduced House Resolution 7599 in 1980 to set aside "wilderness environment . . . where city dwellers can go to experience the solitude" of wild areas. Nearly all of the supporters of the measure included the utilitarian applications of human use of wilderness areas. A prevailing attitude that the land must serve some purpose remains strong in American society, even with a growing understanding of global interdependencies and projected global warming.

The Farris family and their neighbors acted along lines they clearly understood to be "proper" use of the land. Farming, for the early settlers, was a battle to tame the land. It was a battle they eventually lost. Because of the clay under soils, farming the land proved impracticable. Today, much of the land lies fallow or in pasturage, pine trees and oaks reclaiming the land. The Farris land has fairly well "reverted to the forest" as has much of the land harvested by the timber companies during the 1930s. Beaver still inhabit West Sandy Creek, wild hogs still root through the forests, and an occasional deer grazes in the pastures with cattle. But the springs are gone, and the wetlands are dry.

What overall impact has man had on the land? Only future studies will determine how deeply human action has impacted the land. For now, the Farris property appears to have returned to a state of harmony with the surrounding region, unprofitable though it may be.

CHAPTER 11

Folk Toys and Games of Early Texas Settlers

By Kristine McCoy

The people who settled in Texas in the early nineteen hundreds were imaginative and creative in rebuilding their lives in these distant lands. Familiar neighborhoods, friends and family had been left behind for the promise and adventure of new beginnings. The dream of a happy home was pursued with determination, hard work, and extraordinary ingenuity. These settlers, forced to leave most of their talismans and objects of comfort behind, learned to rely on the materials nature provided.

To set up housekeeping, items that were once purchased in stores now had to be made by hand within the home. Men, women, and children learned to make candles, soap, quilts and rugs. Tools and other objects were woven out of straw, sewn from leather, and carved out of wood. Children used their imagination in creating rhythm and guessing games. They played with homemade toys which were meant to entertain the users while teaching a skill. These toys came in all shapes and sizes and are known today as folk toys.

Folk toys can be defined as all those items that are made with natural materials by unskilled craftsmen for personal use rather than for mercantile reasons. They are built in a style that represents the area's culture and are passed down from one generation to the next. The builder may be a loving parent or grandparent creating a toy to please a child. It may be a proud boy or girl proving their ability to create an interesting and challenging object on their own. Natural materials like cornhusks, corn cobs, and sticks could be used to create a doll. Forked sticks could be collected to make slingshot stocks. An old wagon wheel could be pinned to a tree stump to produce a merry-go-round. Such toys, though often primitive in nature, were made to be durable.

Children in the nineteenth century were not showered in an abundance of toys. Therefore, each one they possessed was considered precious. Special care was taken in handling toys because a replacement might be long in coming.

Early Texans placed a great deal of importance on the education of their children even though it was difficult, and sometimes impossible, to send a child to school. Settlements were often widely scattered with no schoolhouse. Parents had to teach their offspring at home, without the aid of the usual books, charts and maps found in the classrooms back East. Certain toys and activities could serve as both a learning instrument and an entertaining distraction to keep youngsters occupied while the adults worked.

The Ball & Cup toy consisted of a wooden cup on a handle with a wooden ball fastened by a length of twine. It tested a child's dexterity as the boys or girls attempted to swing the ball into the cup. The educational aspect of this toy could be expanded by adding a scoring scale which required the users to learn their numbers.

The Climbing Bear was a popular toy used to teach the art of milking the livestock. The wooden bear was hung between two cords. These cords were pulled alternately until the bear reached the top. Another wooden toy similar to the Climbing Bear was the Climbing Sally. This little toy consisted of a wooden board covered in zigzag pegs. Sally, a small wooden figure, was placed at the top of the board and dropped. Her motions as she fell to the bottom slightly resembled those made when climbing. By watching Sally's descent, a child became familiar with the hand and foot combinations needed to safely climb a ladder.

Not all toys and activities were shared by both boys and girls. A young boy was expected to be wilder by nature and therefore his toys and games emphasized physical abilities as well as survival techniques. Hunting was an important skill needed for survival. Many masculine toys were created to perfect such skills. Native Americans introduced a toy which enhanced a boy's fishing skills. This toy, which consisted of a wooden rod with rings attached by a cord, was similar to the Cup & Ball game. The object of the game was to skillfully thrust the rod to capture as many of the rings as possible. The rod represented a spear, and the rings were the fish.

Weapons played an important part in the upbringing and entertainment of little boys. The amateur weapons they wielded early on proved to be practice weapons for their maturity. Slingshots made out of a forked wooden branch with a leather strap to hold a stone could be used to hurl stones at a great speed and distance. Beanshooters shot beans or paper wads across a room. The beanshooter, which was also known as a blowgun, was a simple hollow wooden barrel with a wooden handle.

Natural dart games with darts made out of pricky-pear needles and spear grass were also common. These darts could usually be found in the brush country of South Texas. The prickly pear darts were collected from the center of the prickly-pear blossom and were a perfect torpedo-shaped structure. Likewise, the spear grass darts were easily obtained wherever the grass grew. These spears had tiny little hairs on them which spoiled one's aim. Those who truly knew how to prepare such a weapon knew to lick off the hairs and spit them out. Boys in North Texas found the blood-weed a good source for a javelin. The weed, when it dried in the fall, grew hard and measured six or seven feet high. With the leaves and stems left on, the weed sailed as smoothly as an arrow.

Homemade guns proved to be a somewhat more complex weapon. One such object was the alder-shrub popgun. This gun was created by removing the pith of a thick alder branch and whittling a plunger to fit the hollow tube of the branch. An object such as a paper wad, was placed at each end of the popgun and the plunger was used to quickly push one piece of paper toward the other. The compressed air would create a popping sound as the ball of paper shot out of the end of the branch. The whiplash gun was used to shoot arrows and was made out of leather and wood. A leather thong was attached to a handle carved from a tree branch, and a knot was tied on the outer end of the thong. The knot was used to slip on an arrow. The user then held the handle in one hand and the arrow tail in the other. With a whipping motion, the arrow was sent flying. These arrows were easily made by whittling shingles into appropriate shape.

Most boys possessed the handiest tool of all—a knife. Without it, the majority of the toys and weapons mentioned could not have been created. In addition, wood carving, or whittling, was a pleasant activity that required talent and creativity. An interesting toy carved out of wood is known as a Jacob's Ladder. To make this toy, a series of wooden blocks were linked together by cloth tapes so that they hinged against each other and created an illusion of tumbling down. The block on the end was held by its edges and tipped to touch the second block, which in turn triggered the tumbling action. At times a penny would be placed in the ladder. When operated the penny would disappear and reappear each time a block tumbled.

Another fun toy, the Whimmydiddle, was made by carving six to ten notches into the body of a hardwood branch. A hole was then drilled into the center and a twig rotor was pegged at the end. Another branch was used to rub against the notches and this caused the rotor to spin. Whimmydiddles were often used as lie detectors.

An entertaining sport unique to boys was the paddle and hoop game. This simple game was easy to prepare as it only required a hoop and stick. The hoop was often a discarded barrel rim or the rim of a wagon wheel. The stick was usually just a simple wooden lath. The object of the game was to roll the hoop while running along beside it. The stick was used to keep the hoop upright as the player ran. If the hoop was large enough, the competition could include running through the hoop while it rolled. In this case, the boy who managed to make the most passes through the rim before the hoop fell over won the game.

The outdoor sport known as Indian Stickball was a popular Native American game. This sport, which is often called the roughest sport in the world, required the players to carry or throw a tiny, leather-covered ball between a goal line marked by willow sticks on a field about one hundred yards long. Each team had ten players who followed certain rules. No player was allowed to pick up the ball with his hands but had to use his stick. Once the ball had been picked up, the player could carry it in his hands or teeth. There were no time-outs or substitutions and no time limits. Biting, pushing, gouging, scratching, and hitting with sticks was common. If a player was knocked out his opponent also had to leave the game. The sticks, which resembled today's tennis racket, were carved out of hickory and strung with rawhide thongs.

In the nineteenth century, boys enjoyed rough and tumble playing, but such activities were not considered suitable for girls. Girls were expected to be quiet and graceful. Decorum was their first priority. They were supplied with healthy, sensible work and amusement for leisure hours that would refine their tastes and ambitions. With this in mind, girls focused on activities that honed their homemaking skills while allowing them to remain lady-like. Such activities included sewing, playing house, and playing schoolmistress. House and school acts could involve the help of another child or the use of one's dolls. No matter which was used, the objective was to prepare a girl for the roles of homemaker and mother.

A girl's sewing and stitching activities also prepared her for adulthood. Sewing, rug hooking, making lace, crocheting, and knitting were just a few of the needle crafts young girls spent their time doing. Items such as clothing, curtains, and chair covers were made this way. Performing these chores could be fun as well. Many children were given samplers of linen on which were drawn the alphabet, numbers and pictures. As the child learned how to embroider, she also practiced her letters and numbers. Often, as the young girl advanced in skill, she would begin to sew bible verses on her samplers.

In her memoirs, Mathilda Doebbler Gruen Wagner wrote, "The first doll I ever had, my father cut out of wood. The arms were put on with wire. The hands were just little fists . . . we were pleased with our wooden dolls and thought they were lovely." These words prove that no matter how simple the doll's appearance, they were objects greatly cherished by their owners. They proved useful in the upbringing of little girls. They inspired her imagination and allowed her to practice her motherly duties. Dolls were cuddled, fed, scolded and kissed. They could represent pupils in a classroom or become the best friend of a lonely child. Some creative mothers dressed their dolls in the costumes of different nations. Giving special care to a doll's clothing inspired young girls to appreciate the need to carefully tend to their own clothes as they grew older. All these useful duties involved in caring for one's doll made dolls one of the most important toys found in a child's toy box.

The dolls that early Texans were familiar with varied in many different ways. Some dolls lacked arms and legs, others, faces. They could have naturally made clothing, such as corn husks, or dresses made of cloth. Rough dolls were those made from natural materials such as corn husks, corn cobs, pinecones, straw, acorns, nuts, sticks, grass, and feathers. These dolls were simple to make.

The popular corn husk dolls introduced by Native Americans required the doll maker to roll and pin wet husks into the shape of a person. The doll's skirt had several layers that were squared off so the doll could stand on its own. Corn silk was used to make the hair and was left straight and flowing or was braided. The doll's clothing was also made out of husks. Importance was not placed on the need for facial features with these dolls. However, faces could be applied by using nuts for eyes and noses, or by drawing the features in with charcoal and dyes.

Dolls made out of cloth were popular among girls intent on cuddling and mothering. These dolls, made entirely out of cotton, were softer and more satisfying. They could be made out of a single piece of cloth, rope, or a variety of rags. With a handkerchief, an abstract baby in a blanket was formed folding the cloth to make the baby, while using another fold in the cloth to create the blanket. A piece of cloth could be fashioned into the head, body, and bonnet of a doll. Arms for this doll were simple knots and a dress was made with the rest of the cloth. A head would be stuffed with cotton or a large nut. Facial features, though not always present, could be embroidered or drawn. When sewn, black thread was used for the eyes and red thread for the mouth. At times, buttons or nuts could be used as well. The doll's hair could be fashioned out of yarn, sewn onto the head, and styled to match the little girl's hair.

Wooden dolls, designed to be manipulated or admired, could be crafted out of a single block of wood or carved with more skill with moveable parts. Clothes and spools could be strung together, wooden blocks could be dressed, or wireless clothespins could be fashioned into a human figure. These dolls often represented religious figures like Santa Claus.

An interesting example of an animated wooden doll is the Dancing Man or Limber Jack doll. This toy had a carved wooden figure with arms and legs fastened loosely with pins. The doll was then suspended by a stick or hung on a cord. When the figure was held on a board and the board was tapped, the arms and legs moved in a dancing motion. This little doll was usually left unpainted though some were painted completely black to represent a black dancer.

As with all dolls, wooden figures represented a variety of ethnic groups. Evidence of one's cultural background could be found in the color of the dye used to paint a doll's face. The style of clothing the doll wore also indicated ethnicity.

When girls preferred to play outside, they could engage in games like Hoops and Graces, Leap-Frog-Leap, and the all too familiar

Pat-a-Cake. The game of Hoops and Graces was designed to instruct girls in lady-like behavior. Girls playing the game each held two pointed sticks, crossed at the tips. A medium sized hoop, often decorated with colorful ribbons, was tossed from one girl to another. The object of the game was for each girl to toss and catch the hoop on their sticks while remaining in place and using graceful motions. The game became more challenging as the girls widened the space between them.

Leap-Frog-Leap and Pat-a-Cake were singing games that required just enough physical action to be suitable for little girls. In the frog game, a group of girls formed a circle while squatting on their heels. The point of the exercise was to attempt to hop after each other while in the circle in the manner of a frog and singing "Leap-Frog-Leap." Children today are familiar with Pat-a-Cake, a common diversion that involves a simple clapping routine and singing "Pat a cake, pat a cake, baker's man; that I will master, as fast as I can."

Folk games that involved guessing, rhyming and chasing had a universal appeal and were often performed by both boys and girls. These games encouraged children to compete while working as a team. Some were more intellectual than physical, and others required the use of objects like marbles and horseshoes. The majority of them have been faithfully passed down, generation after generation, and are still heard and seen on our playgrounds today.

Hully Gully, Counting Out, and the Paper-Rock-Scissors were popular forms of intellectual folk games that involved guessing and gambling. Children played Hully Gully in a group and used small objects like nuts and corn kernels. Each child received an equal number of nuts or kernels with which to play. The first child in line held a selected number of nuts or kernels in his hand and the second guessed how many there were. If the guesser was correct, he or she kept the nuts. If the child was wrong, he had to subtract the difference between the correct number and the number guessed. The nuts subtracted were then given to the first player and the process was repeated down the line until a player had collected all the markers.

The Counting-Out game and the Paper-Rock-Scissors games were used as a means to fairly include or exclude a player from being "It." Counting-Out rhymes involved counting, tapping or hand slapping and often had ethnic connotations that targeted groups like the Irish, Blacks, and Jews. Children today would probably be more familiar with rhymes such as Eeny Meeny Miny Moe, and One Potato, Two Potato, Three Potato, Four.

Some of the more physical games enjoyed by early Texans were Indian Wrestling, King of the Mountain, and Wolf Over the River. Catching games, like Wolf Over the River, often required a simple tap on the shoulder or head, or taking a player's handkerchief. In this particular version, two lines were placed between two opposing teams. The player chosen as the wolf stood in the middle of the lines and started the game by yelling "Wolf over the river! Catch all you can!" Each team then tried to run across the other's line and the wolf tried to catch them in between by patting them on the back three times.

Indian Wrestling, which in no way resembles the popular wrestling shows seen today, came in a variety of different forms. Some children thumb wrestled, and others arm wrestled. Another method involved standing toe to toe while holding hands to attempt to pull one's opponent off balance. Sometimes the players stood in a circle with their arms crossed and used their bodies to push each other out of the boundary. Each of these games allowed a child to prove physical dominance. Likewise, the King of the Mountain game illustrated the struggle to prove physical strength. In this game, a player defended territory, usually a small sand hill, from the attack by an opponent.

It is important to note that rhyming games, though constant in their objectives, often varied in content due to cultural differences the English game London Bridge is Falling Down was transformed into the Mexican version of *La Puerta esta Quebrada*, and the German version *Zieh Durch.* A German game of tag, *Boegel Zu Verkaufen,* was quite popular in areas such as Fredericksburg and New Braunfels.

Mexican children along the southern border happily played *Maria Blanca*.

Many toy collections in the nineteenth century included tops, marbles, and noise makers. Tops were carved out of hardwoods and could be decorated in patterns associated with the owner's cultural background. They required practice and skill and could be used for personal satisfaction as well as group competitions. It was not uncommon to find children engaged in a spirited game of Shinny. This game, which resembles the sport Hockey, was set up with a wooden puck, goal lines, and tops. Each player tried to push the puck over his opponent's goal by hitting it with the spinning tops.

Tops of various styles could be used. Those common to the time were the whirly top and the spinning top. Whirly tops, also known as finger tops, were simple little tops spun with a finger. The spinning top was a cone-shaped, wooden toy that was spun by wrapping a string around it and throwing it toward the ground.

Some of the easiest noise-making toys to make were the buzz saw, whistle, and corn stalk fiddle. The buzz saw, which had a round piece of wood with a cord run through it, was a favorite among young boys. When the string was pulled on both ends, the wood spun, making a buzzing sound. Those intent on teasing were fond of catching a girl's long hair with the saw. The whistle was a simple instrument carved out of a willow or elder branch. The branch was hollowed out and the bark was notched to create a vibrating reed. A shriller tone could be produced if a blade of grass was stretched tight in the notch. The slightly more complex corn stalk fiddle was fashioned out of a dry corn stalk and a block of wood. The corn stalk was cut with a knife to create strings out of the natural ridges and the block of wood served as the rosin. All three handmade instruments were guaranteed to make a racket.

Marbles, a well-known game that perfected one's hand and eye coordination, can be considered one of the oldest games ever played. The history of marbles dates back to ancient Egypt and they are commonly associated with gambling games. The marbles themselves have come in many shapes, colors and sizes. Clay, quartz, jasper, tiger eye, marble, crockery, glass and metal are just some of the materials used to make marbles. In Texas, a common source for marbles was agate. This rock, which is a variety of chalcedony, was prized as a source of trade by Native Americans. It is found almost everywhere and became a popular type of marble.

Games with marbles could be simple or complex. Spans and Snops is considered the simplest of marble games. In it, each player shoots a marble with the intention of hitting or nearly hitting the marble belonging to the other players. Players can expand on this by pitching the marbles instead of shooting them with the fingers. If this is done the game is called Bost- About.

For a greater challenge players could engage in the game Increase-Pound. For this game, a circle was drawn in which the players placed their marbles. At a distance from the circle a line is drawn from behind which each player shoots a marble into the circle. The intent is to knock as many marbles out of the circle as possible. After each player has shot from the line, the players continue from the edge of the circle. Each marble shot out of the ring was kept by the shooter. Anyone who hit an opponent's taw, or shooting marble, was forced to place the marbles he won back in the circle. Regardless of the level of difficulty in the games, anyone of them provided hours of fun for children.

It is apparent that as diverse as the population was in Texas in the nineteenth century, one thing shared by all was the desire to create toys and games that inspired a child's imagination while providing hours of fun. In an age before televisions and computers, simplicity proved highly effective at entertaining children. Every wooden toy and doll, no matter how rough in nature, was built with love and cherished for years. The early settlers celebrated creativity and taught children important skills needed for adulthood. As a whole, folk toys and games are traditions that every Texan can share and remember with pride.

BIBLIOGRAPHY

Abernathy, Francis Edward, ed., *Texas Toys and Games,* The Texas Folklore Society XLVIII (Denton: University of North Texas Press, 1997), p. 1, 45, 53.

Additions to the national wilderness preservation system: joint oversight hearings before the Subcommittee on Public Lands, Committee on Interior and Insular Affairs, and the Subcommittee on Forests, Committee on Agriculture, House of Representatives, Ninety-sixth Congress, first session on U. S. Department of Agriculture's RARE II review and recommendations, United States Congress, House Committee on Interior and Insular Affairs, Subcommittee on Public Lands (Washington, D. C.: U.S. Government Printing Office, 1980) p. 59.

Baker, D. W. C. *A Texas Scrap-Book: Texas and its People* (New York: A. A. Barnes and Co., 1875, pp. 568.

Baldwin, John W. "An Early History of Walker County, Texas: A Thesis," Sam Houston State Teachers College (Huntsville, Texas, 1957), p. 17.

Beard, Lina and Adelia, *The American Girl's Handy Book,* with a forward by Anne M. Boylen (New York: Scribner, 1887; reprint, Jaffrey, New Hampshire: David R. Godine, Publisher, Inc., 1987), xxiv.

Child, Lydia Marie, *The Girl's Own Book* (New York: Carter, Hendee and Babcock, 1834; reprint, Bedford, MA,: Applewood Books, 1992) p. 74, 75.

Clark, William, *The Boy's Own Book* (Boston: Munroe and Francis, 1829; reprint, Bedford, MA.: Applewood Books, 1996), p. 9.

Collier, G. Lloyd, "Evolution of Cultural Patterns in East Texas," *Texana II: Cultural Heritage of the Plantation South* (Austin, TX: Texas Historical Commission), p. 2, 4.

Crews, D'Anne McAdams, ed. *Huntsville and Walker County, Texas: A Bicentennial History* (Huntsville, TX, Sam Houston State University, 1976).

Douglas Parish Register, p. 104, also family records in possession of Mr. R. M. Faris of Winchester, Tennessee.

Estill, Harry F. "The Old Town of Huntsville," *Bicentennial History,* ed. D'Anne McAdams Crews for Heritage Committee, Bicentennial Commission of Huntsville (Huntsville, Texas: Sam Houston University Press, 1976), p. 20.

Farris, Mrs. Alton B. "Farris Chapel Methodist Church," 1966, unpublished paper in possession of Farris family, Huntsville, Texas.

Farris, Eva Mae, "Hezekiah Farris Family," *Walker County History* (Huntsville: Walker County Genealogical Society and Walker County Historical Commission, 1987), p.146, 653.

Franklin County Census, Tennessee, Census of 1830, lists "Mrs. Matilda Stevens Roberts."

Franklin County Records, and information in the Bible record as kept by descendants of John Faris. Noted in Edythe Rucker Whitley, genealogists, in *Faris Lineage, Compiled and Researched* (Nashville, privately published, n.d.), p. 12.

General Land Office, *Abstracts of All Original Land Titles Comprising Grants and Locations to August 31, 1941* (Austin: General Land Office, 1941), p. 1047.

Gray Family Bible, in possession of Farris family, Huntsville, Texas.

"Historic Huntsville—From Pleasant to the Present" City of Huntsville, Texas; *http://ci.huntsville.tx.us/cityinfo.html.*

Holet, John Madsden, "A Preliminary Ecological and Herpetological Survey of Walker County, TX," Unpublished thesis, Sam Houston State Teachers College, Huntsville, Texas, 1949.

Hollon, W. Eugene and Ruth Lapham Butler, eds. *William Bollaert's Texas* (Norman, OK: The University of Oklahoma Press, 1956), pp. 290-291.

Jordan, Terry G. *Texas Log Buildings: A Folk Architecture* (Austin: University of Texas Press, 1978), p. 15.

Kalman, Bobbie, *Home Crafts*, Christine Arthurs and Marni Hoogeveen, eds. (New York: Crabtree Publishing Company, 1990), p. 14, 15.

Kearse, Jimmy Farris, "History of the Farris Chapel," paper in possession of the Farris family, undated, p. 1, 2, 3.

Larson, Francis Baker, "Family Pride" (Los Angeles, California, 1996), p. 26, 32.

Leftwich, Rodney L. *Arts and Crafts of the Cherokee* (Cherokee, N.C.: Cherokee Publications, 1970), p. 91.

Louisa County, Virginia, County Circuit Court Records, Anne C. Long, Deputy Clerk. Marriage bond signed by William Shelton. The 1804 Land Book of Louisa County provides documentation that Richard Faris paid $18.00 on 75 acres of land.

Maxwell, Robert S. "The Pines of East Texas: A Study in Lumbering and Public Policy, 1880-1930," *Eastern Texas History: Selections from the East Texas Historical Journal,* ed. Archie P. McDonald (Austin: Jenkins Publishing Company, 1978), p. 156.

Maxia Farris (interview), July 19, 2001, July 10, 2001, Huntsville, Texas.

McFarland, Mrs. I. B., "A History of Huntsville," *The Huntsville Item,* March 6, 1941.

McFarland, Mac, "A History of Huntsville," Bicentennial History, p. 263.

Newcomb, W. W. Jr., *The Indians of Texas: From Prehistoric to Modern Times* (Austin: University of Texas Press).

Park, Mary Francis, *Huntsville and Walker County, Texas* (Huntsville: Sam Houston Press, 1976), p. 55.

Reid, Don. Jr, "The Texas State Prison Has Been in Huntsville a Long Time," Bicentennial History, p. 263.

Riley, Glenda, ed. *The Wild West.* Time-Life Books (New York: Warner Books, 1993), p. 53.

Roberts, Madge Thornhall, *Star of Destiny: Private Lives of Sam and Margaret Houston* (Denton: University of North Texas Press, 1993) p. 95.

Schnacke, Dick, *American Folk Toys* (Chelsea, N. C.: Mountain Craft Books, 1996), p. 16-17. 20, 23, 62, 66,

Seale, William. "Andrew F. Smyth: Jasper County Businessman and Farmer, 1817–1879)," *East Texas Historical Journal* (Vol. II, Number 1, February 1964), p. 8.

Sibley, Marilyn McAdams, ed. "Bishop Morris In Texas, 1841-1842," *East Texas Historical Journal* (Vol. III, October 1965, No.2), p. 156.

Smither, John M. "Early Reminiscences of Huntsville," in Bicentennial History, p. 108.

Soils Survey of Walker County, Texas/ U.S. Department of Agriculture, Soil Conservation service and Forest Service in cooperation with the Texas Agricultural Experiment Station, 1979; Maps 50 and 56.

Wagner, Matilda, *Texas Tears and Texas Sunshine: Voices of Frontier Women,* ed., Jo Ella Powell Exley (College Station: Texas A&M University Press, 1985), p. 114.

Walker County, Texas Census, 1850, Walker County Courthouse, Huntsville, Texas.

Walker County Historical Commission, Walker County Genealogical Society (Dallas, TX, 1986).

Walker County Courthouse Records, Huntsville, Tx., Case Files #8, 12, 14, 70, 206, 243, 295, 286.

Walker County Deed Book, Volume 124, p. 518; Book A, p. 209; Walker County Courthouse, Huntsville, TX.

Winters, J. W. "A Narration," in *Heroes of Texas* (Houston: Texas State Historical Association Quarterly, National Bank of Houston, 1931), p. 3.

PICTURES

Students and supporters of the *Cabin Fever* class. (Courtesy of Susan Locklear)

David Parnell and chainsaw attack the Bois d'Arc. (Courtesy of Susan Locklear)

David Parnell and wounded toe with Jason Surmiller (Courtesy of Susan Locklear)

Brian Peterson and Alex St. Peter with axes against the Bois d'Arc. (Courtesy of Susan Locklear)

Melinda Bonnert and Aerin McQuiggin haul out logs while John Turner watches. (Courtesy of Susan Locklear)

Susan Locklear and Todd Aegin prepare to clean thirty years of manure from the cabin. (Courtesy of Susan Locklear)

Dr. Ross Lovell tackles the latrine. (Courtesy of Susan Locklear)

Preparing to tear off the roof with trucks. (Courtesy of Susan Locklear)

Tearing off the roof. (Courtesy of Susan Locklear)

Laura Johnson, SHSU's oldest graduating senior, with (l to r) Mae Tharpe, Carroll Tharpe, Gene Pipes, Ross Lovell and Kristina McCoy.

Lynette Nadeau, our nurse, advisor, counselor and "mother." (Courtesy of Susan Locklear)

Brian Peterson and Alex St. Peter help with building trusses. (Courtesy of Susan Locklear)

Stuart Cox eyes the project with Dr. Crimm and Melinda Bonnett. (Courtesy of Susan Locklear)

Restructuring the roof. (On the ladders) Chris Ortiz, Mac Woodward, Dr. Crimm; (on the ground in front) Stuart Cox and Don Fink. (Courtesy of Susan Locklear)

Joe Soliz and his crew rebuild the collapsed back corner. (Courtesy of Susan Locklear)

Our cabin waiting for its new tenants. (Courtesy of Susan Locklear)

ABOUT THE EDITOR

DR. CAROLINA CASTILLO CRIMM is Professor Emeritus from Sam Houston State University in the History Department. She is a native of Mexico. Her father's ancestors came to Texas from Monterrey in New Spain in 1792 and received a Power and Hewetson grant in Refugio in 1835. She is a member of the DAR on her mother's side. The Gortons came from England to Massachusetts in 1632 and settled in Rhode Island.

Dr. Crimm holds degrees from the University of Miami, Texas Tech, and the University of Texas. Over the past forty years she has taught history in Winter Park, Florida and Biology in Sweetwater, Texas. After six years of teaching biology, she completed a degree in Architectural Preservation at Texas Tech. In 1989, she received a Fellowship to attend the University of Texas where she completed her Ph.D. under the late Dr. Nettie Lee Benson who started Dr. Crimm on a career teaching Mexican Texas. Upon graduation from UT she was hired at Sam Houston State University. She is a member of many historical societies in Texas.

She has written numerous books and articles and her award-winning book *De León: A Tejano Family History* explores the success of the de León family in founding Victoria, Texas. She recently had the honor of speaking at the de León family's 200th anniversary. She has received numerous awards for her teaching including the prestigious Piper Professor Award as one of the "Best Teachers in Texas." She is currently offering tours around Texas and Mexico as part of her company, Historic Tours of Texas. She lives in Huntsville with her husband, Jack.